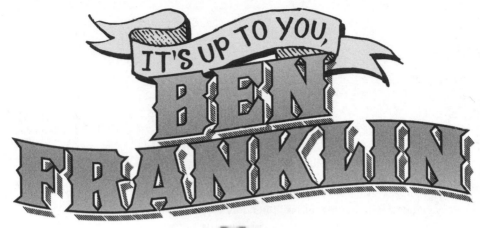

IT'S UP TO YOU, BEN FRANKLIN

TOM AND LEILA HIRSCHFELD

ILLUSTRATIONS BY LISA WEBER
DESIGNED BY NEIL SWAAB

CROWN BOOKS FOR YOUNG READERS
NEW YORK

All rights reserved. Published in the United States by Crown Books for
Young Readers, an imprint of Random House Children's Books, a division
of Penguin Random House LLC, New York.

Image credits are located on page 253.

Crown and the colophon are registered trademarks of
Penguin Random House LLC.

Visit us on the Web! rhcbooks.com

Educators and librarians, for a variety of teaching tools, visit us at
RHTeachersLibrarians.com

Library of Congress Cataloging-in-Publication Data is
available upon request.

ISBN 978-0-553-50949-6 (trade) — ISBN 978-0-553-50950-2 (lib. bdg.) —
ISBN 978-0-553-50951-9 (ebook)

The text of this book is set in 11-point William Text Std.
Interior design by Neil Swaab

Printed in the United States of America
10 9 8 7 6 5 4 3 2 1
First Edition

*For Ben Hirschfeld, who takes after his
namesake in so many good ways*

CONTENTS

AT THE CROSSROADS . . . 1

Choice I—1723 . . . 6
OH, BROTHER!

Choice II—1727 . . . 24
FRESH IN PHILLY!

Choice III—1730 . . . 40
"THE ODD HALF OF A PAIR OF SCISSORS"

Choice IV—1748 . . . 55
ACT TWO

Choice V—1754 . . . 80
UNITED COLONIES OF AMERICA?

Choice VI—1765 . . . 94
DEATH AND TAXES

Choice VII—1772 . . . 116
A "SMALL LEAK"?

Choice VIII—1775 . . . 131
"THERE NEVER WAS A GOOD WAR OR A BAD PEACE"

Choice IX—1778 . . . 156
CELEBRITY, SECRETS, AND SPIES

Choice X—1782 . . . 181
LET'S MAKE A DEAL

Choice XI—1787 . . . 201
LIBERTY FOR ALL?

"LET ALL MEN KNOW THEE . . ." . . . 219

BEN'S FAMILY . . . 225

A TIMELINE OF BEN'S LIFE . . . 227

WHO'S WHO . . . 230

BEN: INNOVATOR AND ORGANIZER . . . 234

BEN: SCIENTIST AND INVENTOR . . . 237

BEN: WRITER AND PUBLISHER . . . 240

RECOMMENDED READING . . . 247

WEBSITES OF INTEREST . . . 251

WHERE TO "VISIT" BEN TODAY . . . 252

IMAGE CREDITS . . . 253

A NOTE FROM THE AUTHORS . . . 254

AT THE
CROSSROADS

YOUR LIFE, BEN, WAS AN amazing journey. Beginning as a poor apprentice, with no schooling past the age of ten, you faced a hard road. But along that road you made unique choices, choices that took you— and America—in new and stunning directions. Who else but you could have achieved all these milestones?

★ **Founding Father:** You're the only person who signed *all* of America's "big four" early documents, including the Declaration of Independence and the Constitution.

Your pen really was mightier than the sword!

★ **Diplomat/spy:** You played a part in the Revolution second in importance only to George Washington's, first getting France's help to win the war and later settling with England to end it.

★ **Scientist:** Your groundbreaking research on electricity established a whole new scientific field, and you shed light on dozens of other topics, from lead poisoning to the Gulf Stream.

★ **Inventor:** You saved countless lives with your lightning rod and low-smoke stove, from which you refused to profit, and delighted mankind with your bifocal spectacles, musical instruments, and other inventions. Oh, and you were the first kitesurfer!

We're spectacular!

Pretty farsighted, Ben!

★ **Writer:** America's leading author of your century, you wrote international bestsellers including *Poor Richard's Almanack* and your famous *Autobiography*.

★ **Entrepreneur:** Starting almost penniless, you worked your way up to control a newspaper, a publishing house, a chain of printing shops, and large real estate holdings.

★ **Civic activist:** You founded America's first lending library and volunteer fire corps, an Ivy League college, a hospital, and many other institutions that improve life for your fellow Americans to this day.

> I never even started college, but I did *start* a college!

★ **Public servant:** You founded and ran the US Postal Service, served Pennsylvania as an assemblyman and later as three-time president of its executive council, and helped write the state's constitution.

Along the way, Ben, you also blazed new trails in understanding what it means to be an American, and you gave America a new image on the world stage. You truly pioneered the American Dream, in which anyone can rise in society through hard work and self-discipline. But how did a humble candlemaker's son from Boston rack up *this* awesome list of achievements? What kind of person does it take to rise from modest beginnings to become one of his country's (and the world's!) all-time heroes?

Okay, maybe you didn't always *seem* so "humble" or "modest." You had a lot to feel pleased with yourself about—and you did. But people still liked you, because you never took yourself too seriously. Of all the Founding Fathers, Ben, you were always the most easygoing, the quickest to smile or crack a joke. That makes you the perfect subject for a biography: not only did you choose one fascinating path after another, but you remembered to have fun along the way.

On your life's voyage, Ben, you faced more than your share of crossroads. Even more than for most people, the decisions you made there changed the world. We're going to take a look at eleven major choices, from how you dealt with your bossy older brother to how you confronted America's deep problem of slavery. At each junction, we'll explore where you were coming from, which ways you *could* have gone, and why you chose the path you did. We're going to walk in your shoes and discover the earthshaking times you lived in, the mind-blowing deeds you accomplished—and the exceptional person you really were. It's not just history, Ben: it's *your* story.

Choice I—1723

OH, BROTHER!

THE CHALLENGE

YOU'RE STUCK WITH THE WORST boss ever—who happens to be your big brother!

THE BACKSTORY

IT'S FUNNY THAT HISTORY WILL remember you as laid-back and grandfatherly, Ben. You may be easygoing, but you also think for yourself. From a very young age, your independent mind has led you to challenge authority.

Of course, what most people don't know is that you're continuing a Franklin tradition. Family lore tells of a long line of rebels who stood up for religious or political freedom:

Your great-great-grandfather, an English village blacksmith, was an activist ahead of his time, spreading the recently outlawed Anglican religion and organizing nearby peasants against unfair land laws. It helped that he knew how to read, which was unusual then.

The first of many Franklins to get into hot water for *writing* was his youngest son, Henry, whose poem insulting a local noble got him tossed in jail for a year.

Then there's *his* youngest son, Thomas II, known for his mechanical genius.

FUN FACT

According to Ben, his great-great-grandfather Thomas Franklin kept his Anglican Bible tied to the underside of a stool. He'd read it to his family on the sly, ready to flip the stool right side up if anyone came snooping!

Not only did your grandfather possess skill as a surgeon, clockmaker, gunsmith, and scribe, but he transcended England's rigid class system by teaching himself astronomy, chemistry, and history.

His youngest son—see a pattern?—your dad, Josiah, rejected the (now-lawful) Anglican religion to become a (not-so-lawful) Puritan, soon after which he ditched England for the colony of Massachusetts. Boston, its capital, was a town of Puritans, so called because they wanted to practice a plainer, "purer" faith, and of other austere Protestants. Boston's elite were known for strict religious observance, solemn dress, sober manners, and low tolerance for new ideas. Josiah did well in Boston selling cleanliness and light: he made soap and candles.

Josiah married your mom, Abiah Folger, the youngest (naturally) of Peter Folger's nine children. Peter was a freethinker through and through. He crossed class lines by marrying a serving maid; left Boston for Nantucket Island, where he taught school and converted local Indians; was jailed for resisting the development plans of wealthy landowners; and wrote a pamphlet during King Philip's War (between Puritans and Indians) in which he claimed God was using the war to punish the Puritans for their intolerance.

Given her upbringing, Abiah must have felt right at home among the nonconformist Franklins. She and Josiah had another trait in common, luckily for you: exceptionally good health. They both lived well into their eighties, a rarity, with no serious illness until shortly before their deaths.

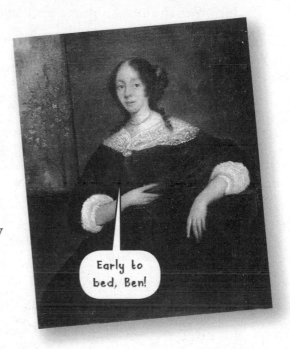

Early to bed, Ben!

A BORN REBEL

SO HERE YOU CAME ALONG in 1706, the *youngest* of your father's sons. (Two sisters came after you, including your lifelong favorite, Jane.) Did your rebellious ways come from your genes, or was it just a family tradition, passed down by a long line of youngest sons? Either way, you grew into a clever, rambunctious lad.

You loved to swim in the river, but were you content to swim like everyone else? Of course not. Observing that kids with bigger hands and feet went faster, you crafted four flippery things out of wood, two with places for your thumbs to grasp and two that tied onto your feet like sandals. Then, somehow realizing that a kite might save you the trouble of swimming altogether, you

used one to glide you all the way across a pond—thus becoming the first known kitesurfer in history! That would not be the last time you came up with a nifty use for kites.

Ben, dude! Far-out idea!

When you were eight, your pious dad decided to raise you to be a minister. You were his tenth son and obviously smart, so he saw you as a kind of tithe (Puritans believe in giving a tithe, or tenth part of their possessions, to the Church). Your path to the ministry would pass through Boston Latin School and on to Harvard College, which was then the only college in Massachusetts.

You had such a promising start, coming in at the top

of your first-year class, that Boston Latin offered to let you skip a grade the following fall. Suddenly, though, your academic glory was cut short. Your dad, deciding that educating you for the ministry would be too expensive, yanked you out of Boston Latin and off the path to college. Instead, he decided, you should take up a trade, so all you got was one more year of basic lessons (at a lesser school, where they taught only writing and math). At age ten, schooling over, you found yourself working in your father's shop: filling soap molds, cutting candlewicks, and skimming the fat off boiling, smelly cauldrons. Bummer.

Disappointed though you were, Ben, you were probably never "reverend" material anyway: you were a little too high-spirited, a little . . . irreverent. As just one example, here's a story told by your sister Jane: you got so tired of the long blessings Josiah would say before *and after* every meal that you made the "helpful" suggestion of saying just one big grace up front, when food was being salted away in barrels for the winter. Your dad was not at all amused by the idea that skipping grace all winter would be a great time-saver.

But fate did not intend you to make candles for long. You hated that work, and your love of adventure began tempting you to run away to sea. One of your brothers had previously done just that, and your dad didn't want a repeat, so he took you around to many different Boston shops, thinking you might like another trade better than his. None seemed a perfect fit, but the tour did show you how lots of different things got made, and this mini-education in manufacturing stayed forever in that unusual brain of yours.

Big Brother Is Watching

AFTER YOU WORKED TWO LONG years with tallow and wicks, your dad found a spot for you as an apprentice to a local printer, who happened to be your older brother James. Josiah pressured you into signing an unusually long contract, promising to stay an apprentice for nine years, by which time you would be twenty-one.

Life was hard for an apprentice: long hours of grunt work for little or no pay, with food and training supposedly a fair reward. James didn't cut his little brother any slack, either, working you at least as hard as anyone else in his shop. There was always more to do: cleaning the floors, cutting sheets of paper, slotting type (pieces of metal, each cast with a letter or two) into heavy trays, spreading ink over the type, or tightening the press to transfer the ink onto the paper. It soon became clear that James wanted you not for your brains but only for cheap labor: he ignored any ideas you offered about what to print or how to print it.

You made the best of a bad situation, continuing your education as best you could without teachers or much free time. First you read your dad's books, mostly ancient or religious texts. Next you made friends with apprentices at the local bookstores, who let you borrow books, but only overnight. Within a few years, you had devoured volume after volume of philosophy, politics, history, grammar, math, logic, and even (still interested in going to sea) navigation.

Your reading taught you many things, including an important lesson you will use often in life: no matter how correct your logic, it won't *persuade* people unless you use it with a light touch. You learned how a philosopher like Socrates, instead of confronting people directly, would approach sensitive issues in a roundabout way, often by asking questions. (You also found that even this method of challenging the common

DIDYA KNOW?

To this day, using questions to persuade is called the Socratic method! Unfortunately, Socrates's actual questions stirred up so much trouble that the Athenians made him drink poison. Pretty harsh!

wisdom could be dangerous: Socrates's fellow Athenians put him to death for it.) To practice different methods of written persuasion, you and a like-minded friend sent letters back and forth on various topics, such as whether women should have an equal right to education.

Okay, but can I ask a few more questions first?

"Silence" Is Golden

AST YEAR, IN 1722, AT age sixteen, you felt confident enough to write some humorous essays, which you decided were pretty good. James had launched a weekly newspaper, the *New-England Courant*, but you guessed he'd be too jealous to publish anything he knew you'd written. So you slipped your first essay under the shop's door one night, written in a script altered to prevent recognition, under the comical pen name of Silence Dogood. The essay claimed you were a middle-aged widow living near Boston, and you had a few things to get off your chest, starting with your life story. (It all began with your birth on a ship carrying your parents here from England; sadly, your fictional dad was still celebrating when a wave washed him overboard.) You didn't expect to please all your readers (you wrote), but you had no plans to displease them, and if anyone took offense— unless you *meant* offense—well, he must not be worth your attention.

Everyone in the shop loved your piece, and James printed it on the front page. Silence Dogood was a hit! You wrote another essay, and another, all poking fun at human foolishness and local problems, and the readers begged for more. James published fourteen Silence Dogood essays in all—until you told everyone who'd written them. Annoyed, he shut you down. As you'll recall, James "thought, probably with reason," that the kudos you were winning "tended to make me too vain." So you got the satisfaction of showing you'd fooled him, but at the price of having poor Silence silenced forever.

In those brief months, you learned to love having fans (even if they had no idea who you actually were). You even got to run the newspaper for three weeks—because James was in prison. True to family tradition, his *Courant* had annoyed the authorities. He complained that the Puritans running Boston thought it was their job to enforce strict morals on *everyone,* regardless of lifestyle or beliefs. James was all for religion, he wrote, but "too much of it is worse than none at all."

Not only that, but, "Of all knaves, the religious knave is the worst"! Seeing the jail time he got for sticking his neck out reminded you once again that gentle humor was safer. His time behind bars did give you valuable management experience, though—and a taste for being in charge.

THE CHOICE

NOW YOU'RE SEVENTEEN, AND JAMES is back in control of the business. He won't publish your essays, he ignores your suggestions, he bosses you around—even hits you when he feels like it—and there's nothing a lowly apprentice can legally do to stop him. It's just not FAIR. After getting shortchanged on your schooling, you're now stuck with a tyrant who won't let you advance at *work*—and beats you when you try!

You could try running away, but that would be disobeying your dad and breaking your contract. How can you win your independence? Do you fight back, continue your education, grin and bear your bad boss, or make a break for it?

A. Hit James back.

Sounds satisfying, though risky. James is older and probably stronger than you. More important, as apprentice you have no legal right to retaliate against your master. He could punish you severely or even have you thrown in jail! It's a tough system, one you'll remember when you hire apprentices of your own, whom you'll treat far more kindly.

Still, fighting back could feel great, at least in the short run.

B. Go to college after all.

At first glance, that door seems closed. Sorry, Ben, but you lack the formal schooling to gain entrance to college, your dad still won't pay for it, and you're legally bound as an apprentice for another four years. And your recent fame as Silence Dogood may not persuade the Puritans who run Harvard to let you in: Silence annoyed the Boston elite by criticizing their hypocrisy and calling for more separation between church and state, so you're not very popular with the powerful these days.

Your essays actually hint that you know perfectly well you're never going to Harvard, all the more frustrating because your richer but less talented Boston Latin classmates have by now enrolled there. Most Harvard students, complains Silence, are "little better than dunces and blockheads," who return from college "as great blockheads as ever, only more proud and self-conceited." Jealous much, Ben? Maybe you *do* want to prove your worth at college after all. . . .

C. Suck it up and serve out your contract.

You've managed to grin and bear it for five years, but can you handle another four? You're practically a grown man now, and you can't stand the way James treats you. You're capable of so much more than he lets you do. Maybe you need to get out and spread your wings!

Although the situation's not all his fault. As you will one day admit, "Perhaps I was too saucy and provoking." You're just not cut out to follow orders blindly, to swallow your pride, to bow and kowtow, to look up to someone who lacks your own ability. It's ironic: under the name Poor Richard, you will one day write, "Let thy child's first lesson be obedience, and the second may be what thou wilt." But obedience was never your own best subject, was it?

D. Run away.

Tempting, though the law's against you. As a sworn apprentice, you'd be "stealing" yourself from your own brother. Of course, once you split, James would have to come catch you, which could be easier said than done. Is skipping town worth the risk?

THE REVEAL

YOU CHOSE . . . **D. Run away.** Hitting back, apart from the risks, simply is not your style. You'd rather avoid a fight by persuading your opponent, compromising, agreeing, pretending to agree, defusing the situation with a joke, or simply backing off. Even as a renowned scientist decades from now, you'll never fight to defend your theories, preferring to let the facts prove you right over time. No one will ever call you macho, but your philosophy of "go along to get along" will allow you to accomplish an awful lot in your eighty-four years.

College is also out of the question, at least for now,

and you won't suffer four more years with James. That leaves you no choice. Exiting Boston is the only way to escape your maddening servitude, but there's another reason to skip town: Boston itself is too narrow-minded a place for you. Your Silence Dogood essays have already made you "a little obnoxious to the governing party," as you'll later put it. You need to find a city that's open to new ideas, a place that will let you be *you,* and Boston is not that place.

So you hop a boat to New York.

THE AFTERMATH

Y OU'RE SO NERVOUS ABOUT JAMES'S finding out and stopping your plan that you have a friend buy your ticket. Once you leave town, though, you take comfort that James is unlikely to chase you: he can't tell people that you're still his apprentice! The reason: Back when the judges sent him to jail, they forbade him to publish, trying to put him out of business. He needed a stand-in (you) to keep the paper going, which meant he had to (pretend to) release you from your apprenticeship, the only way you could legally run the paper.

Secretly, he forced you to sign a letter continuing your contract. Still, he can't exactly use the courts to enforce an illegal letter, can he? So you're safe and bound for friendlier parts.

Now, Ben, the amazing adventure of your life can truly get under way.

FRESH IN
PHILLY!

THE CHALLENGE

CONGRATULATIONS: **YOU'VE MADE IT OUT** from under your brother's thumb. Now that you're finally your own man, you're determined to lift yourself above the ordinary—but how?

THE BACKSTORY

YOUR FIRST CHALLENGE AFTER ESCAPING your brother James was finding a job. William

Bradford, New York's only printer, had no openings, but he took a liking to you and recommended you to his son Andrew Bradford, one of two printers in Philadelphia. (That town's name means "city of brotherly love." Maybe not your favorite topic, given what made you leave Boston?)

Fresh off the boat in Philadelphia, you were not exactly looking your best. Your luggage was still on its way, and the work clothes you wore for traveling were dirty by now, your roomy pockets bulging with extra stockings (men wore those in the 1700s) and even shirts. You spent part of your last dollar on "three great puffy rolls," one of which you tucked under each arm while you scarfed down the third.

Walking along the street, you passed the shop of a carpenter who would end up being your landlord. His daughter, Deborah Read, happened to be at the doorway and (you'll later write) "thought I made, as I certainly did, a most awkward, ridiculous appearance."

Maybe so, but your looks were not all bad; Deborah would become your girlfriend before long. You were tall for the time, about five foot ten, and strongly built, with dark brown hair and an open, friendly expression.

After finishing your puffy rolls, you wandered into a Quaker house of worship and, totally exhausted, fell asleep on a bench. Instead of throwing you out, the kindly Quakers let you sleep, then helped you when you woke, giving you directions to a place where you could spend the night.

You later discovered that Quakers set the tone in Pennsylvania and its capital, Philadelphia, just as Puritans did in Boston. Members of the wealthy Penn family had run the show as proprietors (an old word for "owners") ever since they acquired the colony's land from the king. William Penn paid to make Pennsylvania

FUN FACT

The Religious Society of Friends is referred to as Quakers because their British founder, on trial for blasphemy in 1650, told his judges they should tremble at the word of God. "Quaker" started as a mocking insult but was soon used by many Quakers themselves.

a proprietorship (as opposed to a crown colony, controlled by the king) so that he and other non-Anglicans could worship there free from the persecution they faced in England. Although Philadelphia had fewer people than Boston (only about two thousand when you arrived), it was actually a more dynamic and interesting town, with more opportunities for a nonconformist like you to rise in business and society.

Welcome to Philadelphia, Ben! It's your kind of town.

Young Man on the Rise

YOU BEGAN SEIZING THOSE OPPORTUNITIES the next day and never looked back. Andrew Bradford did not have work for you, but his rival printer, Samuel Keimer, did. Keimer was a somewhat weird boss, often unkempt, rude to customers, and careless in his work, so your diligence and charm made you a welcome addition to his shop. No mere apprentice, you became a valuable assistant—more valuable than he was willing to admit.

Time for a lucky break. A copy of a letter you wrote praising Pennsylvania found its way to the colony's governor, Sir William Keith. Seeking you out, he was so impressed upon meeting you that he decided your abilities were wasted as a mere assistant: he would set you up in your *own* printing business! He gave you a ticket to London, where you could buy the necessary equipment. Money wouldn't be a problem, Keith promised: he would make available all you needed. You were so excited, so confident in your prospects, that you proposed marriage to Deborah before you left, and she became your fiancée.

What an opportunity! Sounds almost too good to be true, doesn't it? Alas, it was: when you got to London in 1724, you found no funds waiting, and they never did materialize. Who knew that Keith had a bad habit of promising more than he could deliver? Decades later, you will still feel the sting of this betrayal by the first powerful man you ever trusted: "What shall we think of a governor's playing such pitiful tricks, and imposing so grossly on a poor ignorant boy!" (Soon angry creditors hounded Keith out of Philadelphia, so at least he got what he deserved.)

Lemons into Lemonade

WITHOUT EVEN THE MONEY TO sail home, you were not only broke but stranded. Luckily, you snagged a job with one of London's largest printers, adding to your knowledge and skills. You found it exciting to be in such a metropolis (over 600,000 people!), with so much intellectual activity (you befriended numerous scientists and published an essay on free will). You kept improving yourself physically as well, swimming for miles in the River Thames and carrying double loads of type trays up and down the printer's stairs.

You found plenty else to like in that bustling city—so much, unfortunately, that in almost two years you wrote to your fiancée only *once*, and that was to notify her that you'd be staying longer than expected.

The many friends you made in London included a Quaker merchant who liked you well enough to offer you a ticket home if you would help him establish a shop for general merchandise in Philadelphia. On the trip back across the Atlantic, being Ben Franklin, you indulged your growing interest in science by making a study of dolphins and flying fish, examining small crabs you found in floating seaweed, and even calculating the distance traveled from London based on your observations during a lunar eclipse.

Two bad things happened after you arrived home: First, Deborah told you she'd dumped you in

DIDYA KNOW?

Those dolphins must have made an impression on Ben. When he later created a family coat of arms, he put a dolphin in the middle!

favor of another guy. Be honest—you deserved that for forgetting about her in London. Second, the Quaker merchant died suddenly after just a few months, leaving you a small sum . . . and no job.

You've managed to land on your feet as usual, though. You've gone back to work for Keimer, but now as print shop manager. You've also shown your ingenuity (and how much you learned in London) by breaking the British monopoly on metal type: instead of importing, like every other American printer, you've set up a mini-factory in Keimer's shop, pouring molten metal into molds you created from the type Keimer already owned. Gee, maybe all that drudgery with soap and candle molds is starting to pay off! For you, Ben, *no* experience is wasted, even if it seems like a drag at the time.

THE CHOICE

SO, YOUR CAREER IS GOING pretty well, considering the challenges you've faced. But you are not the kind of guy to be satisfied with "pretty well." Your ambition drives you to *create* something that will give you a major boost in achieving the kind of success you desire. You want to be part of something bigger than yourself, something that will make a difference in the world, preferably something that *you* begin. But what?

WHAT DO YOU DO, BEN? SELECT ONE:

A. Launch a political party.

At age twenty-one, that would certainly be impressive. And Pennsylvania politics could sure use some shaking up. Now that the idealistic founder, William Penn, has passed on, his sons are selfishly milking the colony for cash. So long as they can keep collecting rent and selling off land parcels to support their lavish lifestyles, they don't show much concern for the average citizen's quality of life, providing little in the way of basic services such as sanitation or fire safety. They and their handpicked officials have been lording it over the Pennsylvania Assembly, the colony's weak legislature. That bothers you.

B. Start a club.

Every schoolkid knows that starting a club can be even more fun than joining one. Founders also get extra respect, something you might enjoy. Could starting your own club in Philadelphia be a cool way to win friends and influence people?

C. Found a church.

Okay, maybe you're not the religious type. As a kid, you felt restless under your father's strict religiosity. As a teenager, you considered the increasingly fashionable notion of rationalism, which puts pure reason before any God, but in the end you did not find it morally satisfying. Now you are leaning toward deism, a kind of churchless belief in an unknowable God that will be quite popular among your fellow Founding Fathers. (Call it *disorganized* religion.) Eventually, you will decide that even deism's not a fit: "I began to suspect that this doctrine, though it might be true, was not very useful."

"Useful" is the key word. As with most other pursuits, Ben, you're interested in religion for the *practical good* it can do. It's not about praying to get what you want or making bargains with God: you can never convince yourself that God answers prayers directly. In 1757, you'll narrowly escape a shipwreck; you will write home that instead of showing your gratitude by building a chapel, you'd rather build a lighthouse. And when a town in Massachusetts names itself Franklin in your honor, in 1778, and asks you to donate a bell for its church tower, you will send books for its library instead, "sense being preferable to sound."

No, rather than look to God for tangible help, you value religion for the comfort it can provide and, even more, for the virtues it can encourage. One big problem you have with Puritanism is its doctrine that people go to Heaven through prayer and God's grace, *not* for their good deeds. For you, good deeds are what life is all about; the best way of serving God is to help His other children. "Sin is not hurtful because it is forbidden," you'll write, "but it is forbidden because it is hurtful."

The kind of religion you like least is the kind that demonizes other beliefs just for being different. Dogma matters far less to you than virtue: "A virtuous heretic shall be saved before a wicked Christian." That helps explain why, when it comes time to draft the US and Pennsylvania constitutions, you will stoutly support freedom of worship and oppose any religious requirements for government office.

D. Establish a business.

Launching a company takes serious money, which you don't have yet. You most particularly don't have enough cash to equip a machine-heavy business like a printing shop. Then again, you've always been gifted at overcoming obstacles. Can you find the start-up capital if you search creatively?

THE REVEAL

YOU CHOSE . . . **B. Start a club.** In all your life, Ben, you will never even formally *join* a church, let alone found one. You'll pay for a pew in your wife's church and donate there in her name, but you will never commit to religion yourself.

You believe all religions are good to the extent that they help people in this world; as to the next world, you cannot say. As you age you will donate money to every church in Philadelphia, plus the Jewish synagogue, and all the town's clergy will one day unite at the head of your massive funeral procession.

As for politicking, you're not really that into it (at least not now). You care about improving your community, but not yet through the political process: you believe ordinary people working together can often accomplish more than government can. So instead, you do indeed start a club. But this is no ordinary club, just as you are no ordinary guy.

THE AFTERMATH

YOU CALL YOUR CLUB THE Junto, from a Spanish word meaning "together." Its nickname is the Leather Apron Club, because the members are basically all tradesmen like you, though mostly older. (Tradesmen like printers and blacksmiths wear leather aprons to keep their clothes cleaner.) You meet at first in a tavern, later renting a building as your clubhouse. From the beginning, though, you maintain a pretty highbrow tone for a group of shopkeepers and artisans. You call it a club "established for mutual improvement," but your goal is also for the members to improve the larger community.

Meetings cover a range of subjects—commercial, political, and philosophical. A few of the many examples you offer as guidelines: What good stories have you heard lately? How can the laws be improved? Do you know any rich man, and if you do, do you know how he got that way? Have you or has any acquaintance been sick? What treatment was used, and what were the results? How can the Junto's other members help you, and vice versa?

The agenda generally covers topics in morals, politics, and science, including steps the citizens of Philadelphia might take together to make life in town better for everyone. The discussions reflect your curiosity about everything in the world, so long as it has some practical value. They also show your distaste for open argument: you set small fines for members who directly contradict or disagree with others. You want to keep meetings pleasant, and you are all trying to practice the refined manners of gentlemen.

Gentlemen? In 1727, the idea that mere tradesmen might act like wealthy, educated "gentlemen" is actually pretty radical: in a world of fixed social classes, you are promoting (gasp) upward mobility—thus helping to set an American precedent. It helps that the colonies have no hereditary nobility and less income inequality than England, but you are determined to remove even more barriers to the rise of the middle class.

What really sets the Junto apart, though, and makes it last for decades, is its dedication to the public good. First you lead your members in gathering books for a shared collection, which evolves into America's first subscription library. You probably wish you'd had one growing up! You wouldn't have been limited to your dad's books or forced to beg overnight loans from other apprentices.

Over time the Junto will lead the fund-raising to establish a Philadelphia police force, America's first volunteer fire brigade, and a college that develops into the University of Pennsylvania. Through the Junto (and, later, when you have your own newspaper), you will end up proposing and achieving nearly every project that makes Philadelphia life better over the next sixty years.

The Junto's many projects will demonstrate a core belief of yours: "The good men may do separately is small compared with what they may do collectively." The experience will also teach you to share credit where possible. If an undertaking is identified too closely with any one person, it's human nature for others to stay away out of jealousy or pride, so the project may fail. With the benefit of experience, you'll advise people to wait before claiming their share of glory for any group success: "The present little sacrifice of your vanity will afterwards be amply repaid."

As for your Library Company of Philadelphia, it will go on to inspire the founding of other libraries throughout America and to thrive for centuries to come. Nice job! Its motto sums up your civic philosophy: "To pour forth benefits for the common good is divine."

Oh, and don't worry about not having start-up capital yet: your time as an entrepreneur will come. Read on!

FUN FACT

The Library Company of Philadelphia is still open to the public today. It served as the Library of Congress until 1800 (when Congress moved from Philadelphia to Washington) and continued as the largest library in the country until the 1850s!

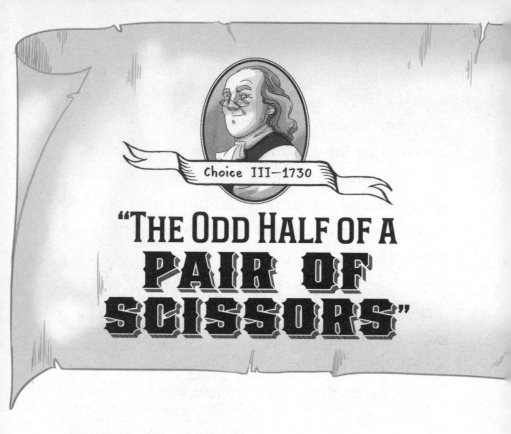

"The Odd Half of a PAIR OF SCISSORS"

THE CHALLENGE

GOOD NEWS: **YOUR BUSINESS CAREER** and public life are off to a strong start. But you've still got to find the right wife—and convince her *you're* the right husband.

THE BACKSTORY

YOU ARE TWENTY-FOUR, AND YOUR star is definitely rising.

Soon after forming the Junto, you got tired of having Keimer boss you around. You also suspected that he was just using you to attract customers and train the younger assistants and was planning to fire you as soon as they knew enough. So you quit first, taking an assistant named Hugh Meredith along as a partner—the only way for you to launch a new shop, because Meredith's father supplied the initial capital. Then Meredith began drinking too much, so you borrowed enough to buy him (and his dad) out. Congratulations! You are finally the proud owner of your very own printing shop.

You've been writing, too. Andrew Bradford, then Philadelphia's biggest printer, also had a newspaper, the *American Weekly Mercury,* which you thought could use some competition. When Keimer heard you wanted to start a newspaper, though, he rushed out his own first, mostly to spite you. So you switched tactics and wrote for Bradford's paper under the name Busy-Body, penning breezy essays that qualified you as America's first known gossip columnist. (And Busy-Body's column often took potshots at Keimer. Coincidence?)

A License to Print Money

KEIMER WAS LOSING CASH AND eventually left town to escape his debts—but not before selling you his paper, which you renamed the *Pennsylvania Gazette*. So now you're a publisher as well as a printer. Bradford's newspaper is outselling yours, however, partly because Bradford's also postmaster and so has better distribution. He even forbids his postmen to carry your *Gazette*! That forces you to bribe them—and you can't afford much, because you still have to pay off the money you borrowed to buy out Meredith.

Meanwhile, you take every opportunity you can to win business. To let everyone see how hardworking you are, you make a big show of personally

Rise of the Spirit of Independence

FUN FACT

Early postal riders carried horns to let people know they'd arrived to pick up and drop off the mail.

wheeling giant loads of blank paper to your shop, rather than having them delivered. You take advantage of any mistakes Bradford makes, printing anonymous letters in the *Gazette* about his typos and poor writing. When he does a careless job printing a speech by the governor to the assembly, you print it correctly and distribute it free to all the assemblymen, a clever move that snags you a share of all their printing business.

You've even started to get involved in politics yourself—to solve a problem, of course. Pennsylvania has a shortage of paper money, which makes the Penns and their wealthy friends happy: they fear that printing more would lower the value of each pound note they already own. But the middle and lower classes need more currency for their daily business, and the population is growing fast. So you publish a pamphlet arguing eloquently to increase the supply of paper money, which influences the assembly to pass a law in favor of an increase. And guess what? The assembly is so impressed that it gives *you* the job of printing the new money. That's an early example of how your writing ability has helped both your business and your political career.

THE CHOICE

IN ONE AREA OF YOUR life, though, you are seeing much less progress. You're courting a young lady, a relative by marriage of Thomas Godfrey, whose family lives in the same house where you are rooming. (Mrs. Godfrey kept singing the young lady's praises until you agreed to meet her.) You like her, too—enough to visit her home quite a few times, until the moment of truth arrives. It's time to discuss the big question: How much will her parents pay you to marry her?

In 1730, Ben, marriage is seldom about love, or at least it doesn't start out that way. It's about making a match that helps both people (or even both families) in a practical way. Sure, attraction and even affection may play a role in choosing a mate, but life is already challenging enough—why rush into a marriage that doesn't make it easier in some way?

Proposing to a woman means promising to support her for life, and the custom is for her family to make a dowry payment to get her off their hands. (Gee, could one reason be that society in the 1700s makes it really hard for women to earn good livings by themselves?) Her parents size up potential grooms, pick the suitor with the best prospects, and sweeten the deal by offering a dowry to help the new couple get started.

DIDYA KNOW?

In some cultures even today, women use dowries to find good husbands. But in other parts of the world, it's the groom who has to pay.

And that's where your romantic plans hit a glitch. You name a dowry you think reasonable, enough to pay off your debts, but the family says they can't afford it. They don't even make a counteroffer, claiming they don't have enough money for *any* dowry. You, trying to be constructive, suggest they could always take out a loan on their house. No dice: *now* they say they've been checking you out, even talking to your competitor, Bradford, and they aren't so impressed with your prospects after all. Can you really support their daughter? Printing's a tough business, you're young, you've got debts, and so on. The deal is off—and don't bother visiting again.

Nice people, huh? You suspect they're trying to stiff you on the dowry. Maybe they think you've already fallen so far in love that you'll now elope, giving up on any payment. That would work out nicely for them, wouldn't it? The young lady seems blameless, and you *do* like her, but would you even want to marry into a family like that? So you don't exactly jump for joy when, a little while later (maybe once it's clear you're not eloping), Mrs. Godfrey brings news that the parents are prepared to reconsider.

Meanwhile, you've stayed in touch with your old fiancée, Deborah, who's had a run of hard luck. Her husband, John Rogers, a potter, turned out to be a bad choice. After she gave up on you and married Rogers, she learned that he might already have a wife in England. She moved back home, while Rogers went off to the West Indies, where he reportedly died in a brawl. There's no proof that he's dead, though, so she's still legally married. Even if she could marry you (and wanted to), her family really is poor, so she definitely comes without a dowry—and those debts of yours aren't going to pay themselves.

Maybe there's another option. You don't know this, but in two years a guy named George Washington will be born. He will become "first in war, first in peace, first in the hearts of his countrymen," but before all that he will be second—second husband to a rich widow, whose fortune will help him achieve all those other things. Could you perhaps find some wealthy heiress to marry, someone who sees your potential and helps you fund your business?

Or should you just

It's as easy to love a rich girl as a poor one, Ben. My wealth certainly helped George.

forget about marrying for now and focus on work? There's certainly plenty to do.

A. Reopen negotiations on the dowry.

There's a reason you were courting this young lady to begin with: you like her. *She* can't help it if she has jerky parents. She's the one you'd be living with, not them. Of course, you'd still have them as in-laws. But you're a persuasive guy, and a good negotiator. They clearly know they over-played their hand, so chances are you could cut a good deal with them. And did we mention that you like her?

B. Find a way to wed Deborah.

Could be tricky. You can't marry legally without proof that her husband either had another wife in England or is dead now, so you'd have to "take her to wife" without making it official. This is called a common-law marriage.

Is it even worth that complication when she has no dowry to offer? She's also not a great beauty, truth be told. She's got a loud voice and a somewhat coarse manner. But you sense that she's got a good heart, and that she could make a good *partner:* she's a hard worker, thrifty and sensible. Also, you pity her "unfortunate situation," which you blame partly on the way you neglected her during your two years off in London. Now you have a chance to correct your mistake, which you always like to do when possible.

C. Get hitched to a wealthy heiress.

Marrying money can actually turn out to be expensive. A spoiled, rich wife might demand a lifestyle too fancy for your simple and practical tastes, even if you could afford it.

Besides, you're no George Washington. Though not born rich, he'll come from an aristocratic family; you may be smart and charming, but by society's rules you're still just a tradesman. No wealthy parents in Philadelphia are going to want their daughter marrying anyone but an upper-class "gentleman."

As your intended's family so rudely told you, printing is not even viewed as a very promising trade. So heiress, shmeiress—you're unlikely to attract a wife with even a decent dowry. Unless, that is, she's got some huge drawback, like an empty head or a nasty temper. There *are* things that matter more than money.

But what if you *could* find someone with all the qualities you want: wealth, frugality, nice looks, and a good disposition? Wouldn't that be fantastic?

D. Forget about marrying for now.

Hey, you're a fun-loving guy who enjoys single life, so why not play the field awhile longer? You could even hold out for a willing heiress. The longer you wait, the more attractive you might become as husband material.

Still, you do have several reasons not to tarry. First of all, marriage will help your business: married men have an image of steadiness and reliability. It's 1730, and customers are not quite ready to trust a man who's still a bachelor past twenty-five or so—and you're now twenty-four. Second, marrying will give you someone to cook and clean for you without pay. Romantic? No, but practical. Third, and more important, you genuinely like the idea of having a partner in life. You believe men belong in settled relationships, later writing that a single man "resembles the odd half of a pair of scissors."

Your fourth reason is the most urgent—and it's a doozy. It turns out you've been enjoying single life a bit *too* much: you have just become a dad. You never reveal the name of your son's mother, but apparently she's no one you feel comfortable marrying or even leaving him with. So not only do you need a wife, but your new baby, William, needs a mother. So will you choose one of your two current prospects, or look (quickly) for someone else?

THE REVEAL

YOU CHOSE . . . **B. Find a way to wed Deborah.** You pick Deborah, partly because you're still furious with the other girl's parents. Later you'll recall that you "resented" them, which is almost as angry as you ever admit to getting. You tell the Godfreys you never want to see their relatives again, and you don't sugarcoat it: the Godfreys themselves move out of your rooming house soon after and don't speak to you for years. (This may be why the young lady's name is lost to history.)

Here's the thing, Ben: despite your calm and easygoing reputation (cultivated in your writing and through long practice at the Junto), you *really* don't like it when people try to take advantage of you. Remember your brother James? When you were eighteen and had earned some money, you went back to Boston and made a point of cruising by his shop in a "genteel new suit." You bragged to his workers, showing off your money and your new watch, while he glowered, turning his back on you. It thrilled you to rub his face in your good fortune. In your own subtle way, you often manage things so that anyone who mistreats you comes to regret it. (To be fair, when James later falls ill and needs help, you will have the good grace to help him, making up for your snarky behavior.)

THE AFTERMATH

YOU NEVER DO THE CHURCH wedding thing with Deborah, yet your marriage is strong enough to last until her death, forty-four years later. She's not a bad mother, either. Though she and William won't always get along, he's much better off than with no mom at all. All in all, marrying Deborah is the right move.

True, she doesn't help you socially. When the gentry later invite you into their homes, Deborah's name will rarely make it onto the guest list. She has little education and even less of your intellectual curiosity. For the rest of her life, while you travel America and roam the courts of Europe, she will never even want to leave Philadelphia.

But she does help plenty at the shop (keeping the accounts better than you did, buying rags for paper-making, stitching together pamphlets, etc.), and she also keeps your home running, so for years you won't need to hire servants. Her talents and good sense will enable many of your later achievements, by freeing you to focus on things other than household and shop matters.

Fine, so your marriage doesn't exactly sound like a grand passion. But that's okay, because *both* of you are practical people. Over time, a deep sense of admiration, even fondness, will grow between you. In your many letters back and forth, you'll often address each other as "My Dear Child," a term of real affection in the 1700s. You'll even publish a lovely poem about your love for Deborah, called "My Plain Country Joan."

Deborah is a fierce, lifelong ally. She may not be an ideal match for you intellectually, but who could be? As Poor Richard, you will advise spouses to tolerate each other's flaws: "Keep your eyes wide open before marriage, half shut afterward."

You're not exactly the ideal match yourself, you know. You can be patronizing ("Don't you know all wives are in the right?") and bossy (advising every woman to "honor and obey" her husband). One of your favorite virtues is frugality, not to say cheapness, which you will expect of Deborah even after you become rich. And you'll end up spending fifteen of her last seventeen years away from home, not all by necessity, even when she writes how much she misses you.

So which of you is getting the better part of this marital bargain?

Choice IV—1748

ACT
TWO

THE CHALLENGE

YOU'RE HAPPILY MARRIED TO DEBORAH, your family is thriving, and you've earned more than enough money. But what do you do with your life now that you've already found success?

THE BACKSTORY

THE FRANKLIN HOUSEHOLD SOON GREW from three to four, when Deborah gave birth to your son Francis. Everyone loved Franky, a clever and lively lad who took after you even more than William did. You and Deborah spent many happy hours with the adorable tyke. When Franky was four, though, tragedy struck: he died of smallpox—shortly before you were planning, with terrible irony, to have him immunized against the disease.

This awful blow was one of your life's worst. "When nature gave us tears," you wrote soon after, "she gave us leave to weep." You generally pride yourself on not letting regret for past losses cloud your future happiness, Ben, but *this* pain will never fade completely. Even thirty-six years later, you'll admit to your sister Jane (your favorite correspondent ever, judging by the number and intimacy of your letters), "to this day, I cannot think of [Franky] without a sigh."

Some light did come into your life with the birth of your next and last child, Sarah (affectionately known as Sally). You're making sure she grows up a Franklin, learning not only the usual household arts but also business skills such as accounting. She is a good daughter, dutiful and loving (though not very intellectual), and she will give you much comfort in your later years.

I'd like to think I take after Mom.

MEDIA MOGUL

YOUR BUSINESS, MEANWHILE, HAS FLOURISHED. The *Gazette* has risen steadily in circulation, lifted by a mix of serious news, crime stories, jokes, spicy gossip, and even an advice column. Unlike your brother James, you try not to play politics in your newspaper, so you usually avoid offending the authorities or losing readers. Your credo as publisher: "When men differ in opinion, both sides ought equally to have the advantage of being heard by the public." You also believe printers should be evenhanded and "cheerfully service all contending writers that pay them well, without regarding on which side they are of the question in dispute." You set a great example for Americans, Ben, of openness to discussing new ideas.

Your low-key approach, which will also influence your style as a politician, has already helped you make and keep powerful friends. *They* helped dislodge your publishing competitor, Bradford, from his job as Pennsylvania postmaster when his careless record keeping caught up with him. You got the position, which lets you reach more readers—and there's no more need to bribe the postmen! Because you like to play fair, you do not shut Bradford's *Mercury* out from the mail, as he did with your *Gazette*.

Your printing house is big enough to employ many assistants, which has given you the chance to do a good deed for your brother James. Sick and out of work, he wrote begging you to hire his ten-year-old son, so you did—making "ample amends" for running out on your brother all those years ago. (Just as you like getting even when someone does you wrong, you often try to make up later for behavior you regret.)

Your many trainees also provide the raw material for yet another Franklin innovation: franchising! Once you're satisfied by their character and skills, you set them up in business elsewhere: Connecticut, South Carolina, even the Caribbean. In return for your start-up equipment and ongoing written content, they agree to send you a share of their profits. Before you're done, you'll have set up twenty-four of these offshoots, part of a business empire that also includes the *Gazette*, book publishing, and your almanac.

Who knew fast-food chains were following in Ben's footsteps?

Ah, yes, your almanac. Started in 1732, it comes out once a year and, like most almanacs, offers weather forecasts and calendars of holidays and astronomical events. That's not why most people buy it, though, instead of its competitors. They buy it for your writing, or rather the writing of "Richard Saunders," a not-too-sharp alter ego you dreamed up. "I am excessive poor," you explained (as Richard) in the first issue, and "the printer has offered me some considerable share of the profits." In 1736, "Poor Richard" stoutly denied rumors that he was really you: "My printer, to whom my enemies are pleased to ascribe my production . . . is as unwilling to father my offspring as I am to lose the credit of it." *Poor*

Richard's Almanack is now a huge bestseller, selling as many as ten thousand copies per year.

Every year, Poor Richard amuses the world with offbeat ideas and tales of his latest troubles. He also fills the margins and empty calendar days with little sayings, some original but many lifted (with improvement) from earlier writers (who often did the same themselves). Poor Richard's witty advice (which neither he nor you always follow) is fast earning a permanent place in American wisdom. Just a few examples:

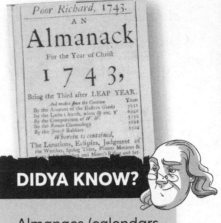

DIDYA KNOW?

Almanacs (calendars with astronomical data) have been around for over three thousand years! Experts believe the term may come from Arabic, like other mathy words such as "algebra" and "algorithm."

★ Early to bed and early to rise makes a man healthy, wealthy, and wise.

- ★ He that lies down with dogs shall rise up with fleas.
- ★ God helps them who help themselves.
- ★ No gains without pains.
- ★ Haste makes waste.
- ★ Little strokes fell great oaks.

PENN PALS? HARDLY!

WHILE YOUR BUSINESS HAS BEEN growing, so have your social connections. Your many community projects serve not only to help others, a crucial goal in your life, but also to help you. For example, a wealthy landowner who agrees to lend a rare book to your library is much friendlier afterward: as you later write, "He that has once done you a kindness will be more ready to do you another, than he whom you have yourself obliged." Sadly, this "Ben Franklin effect" (as psychologists will one day call it—seriously) does not apply to Pennsylvania's biggest honchos, the Penn family, who initially donated to the library. *They* do not like you anymore.

To be fair, they have their reasons. Thomas Penn, head of the family since the death of his father, William, has moved back to London and abandoned his dad's Quaker religion for the Anglican Church, which is still tops in England. British persecution of Quakers, remember, was the main reason William founded Pennsylvania in the first place. *Thomas* seems to care little about the colony (except for the land rents he collects), and he doesn't want a strong local government there (it might challenge his authority). You disagree firmly on both counts.

Thomas, I'm so disappointed in you.

You *do* care about your fellow citizens: in 1736, you helped established the Union Fire Company, America's first volunteer fire department. At the same time, you want to strengthen the Pennsylvania Assembly, which currently has little power against the Penns. For that purpose, you used your connections (also in 1736) to get appointed clerk of the assembly, which means you hear and record every action taken there. (Handy info for a newspaper publisher!)

The assembly is divided between the Penn faction and everyone else (mostly Quakers and recent German immigrants). You're not a big fan of the Penns and their rich friends: instead, you favor the "middling people," the tradesmen and farmers who actually get stuff done. What's really ticked the Penns off, though, is the citizens' militia you formed last year, in 1747.

As with so much in America, it all started with the Indians. (It will be two centuries before they are known as Native Americans.) William Penn tried to treat them with relative fairness, negotiating land treaties and sticking to those treaties, but his son Thomas has been cheating the Indians at every opportunity. He often lays phony claim to their land, rents it quickly to settlers, then lets the *settlers* try defending it from the outraged tribes. And if the poor settlers have to flee their farms, he keeps charging them rent! So everyone loses but Thomas. Now his crooked game is getting harder, because French agents are sneaking down from French-held Canada (along the western frontier) to stir up trouble. These agents recently began encouraging more Indian raids against English settlers—even on land covered by legitimate treaties.

The Penn faction wasn't doing much to mobilize a defense, the British army was elsewhere, and the Quakers were pacifists. How could rural farmers protect their families from attack and promote peace with the Indians? Ben Franklin to the rescue! You organized a lottery that raised enough money to equip a militia. You even wrote the militia association's charter, whose defiant tone foreshadows a certain famous declaration: "Being thus unprotected by the government under which we live, we do hereby, for our mutual defense and security . . . form ourselves into an Association."

Your militia beat back the French threat (for now) and disbanded, but the Penns are still furious with you. "This association is founded on a contempt to government . . . a part little less than treason," Thomas wrote to a henchman. If people could act "independent of this government, why should they not act against it?" He recently complained of you, "He is a dangerous man, and I should be very glad he inhabited any other country, as I believe him of a very uneasy spirit." The Penns hate the way you seem capable of taking government into your own hands, but for now they don't oppose you outright, because you are too popular.

Geeking Out

WHEN NOT SAVING THE COLONY or annoying the Penns, you have also been spending much time on science, which you call natural philosophy. You are curious about *everything*. You study how dark fabrics absorb more heat from the sun (you put different-colored swatches on snow and see how much it melts), how the big storms called nor'easters actually travel up the coast from the *south* (you track them by the times of day they hit different cities, as reported in local papers), how comets come to be, how blood circulates, how oil interacts with water, and on and on and on.

You're not interested in abstract theory for its own sake: all your work has a purpose. Some is purely for fun, such as your amazing "magic squares" of numbers, where all the rows, columns, and major diagonals add to the same sum. You play with these during idle moments in the assembly, creating megasquares, up to sixteen by sixteen, in which no number appears more than once ("the most magically magical of any magic square ever made by any magician"). But almost all your research is meant to serve some practical goal: in your words, "What signifies philosophy that does not apply to some use?"

6	7	2
1	5	9
8	3	4

When you confirm that dark fabrics absorb more heat, for example, you *use* the data to recommend that people traveling to hot climates pack light-colored clothes, while farmers who want to ripen fruit quickly should store it in dark-painted sheds. You aim to serve humanity, refusing to milk your discoveries for cash. Pennsylvania's governor (though appointed by the Penns) even offers you an exclusive patent on your safe, efficient Franklin stove, but you turn it down: "As we enjoy great advantages from the inventions of others, we should be glad of an opportunity to serve others by any invention of ours, and this we should do freely and generously." What a guy!

In 1743, you created the American Philosophical Society, whose very name ("American") demonstrates your unusual sense of the many colonies as a single entity. (Most organizations until now have served one colony or another, not all the colonies.) For centuries to come, this society will bring scientists together on local and national levels, spreading knowledge and pushing back the boundaries of ignorance.

Nobody's Perfect

MEDIA MAGNATE, MEGAPRINTER, BESTSELLING author, leading citizen, noted scientist: amazing as all this is, for you it's not enough. You believe you could be doing even more with your life.

Soon after marrying, for example, you embarked on a "Project for Moral Perfection." The plan: to master twelve important virtues, including order, frugality, industry, sincerity, and tranquility. A friend advised you to add one more virtue you lacked—humility—and you had to admit he was right. Because thirteen virtues might be too much to practice at once, you decided to focus on one per week, so each virtue would get four weeks per year. You kept track in a notebook, one page per week, with a "little black spot" marked for each slipup, like a demerit. Gosh, those little spots sure began to add up!

Before long, you realized that the goal of perfection was impossible. The virtues giving you the most trouble were order (you were never a clean-desk kind of guy) and especially humility. "I cannot boast of much success in acquiring the *reality* of this virtue, but I had a good deal with regard to the *appearance* of it," you later confessed. You could not overcome pride completely: "Disguise it, struggle with it, beat it down, stifle it, mortify it as much as one pleases, it is still alive, and will every now and then peep out and show itself." The task, you saw, was hopeless: even if you succeeded somewhat, "I would probably be proud of my humility."

Admitting failure, you consoled yourself that no one likes a goody-goody anyway: "A perfect character might be attended with the inconvenience of being envied and hated." So much for moral perfection! But now, at the age of forty-two, you decide your life still needs an upgrade. Something big has got to change. To make that happen, you announce . . . your retirement.

THE CHOICE

WAIT, YOUR *RETIREMENT*? HOW COULD you, the original workaholic, just up and retire? Sure, you can afford it: you've been investing your business profits in Philadelphia property, so the city's growth has helped make you one of the wealthiest men in the colony. And some business owners do retire in their early forties, particularly given that old age and illness often arrive by that age in the 1700s. But *you're* still in good health—only halfway through your life, as it turns out. Why not just keep expanding your media and real estate empires and get even richer?

Here's why: to you, money is just a means to an end: "The use of money is all the advantage there is in having money." As with science (and religion), you believe the main purpose of wealth is to assist in doing good: "I would rather have it said, 'He lived usefully,' than, 'He died rich.'" If anything, having too much money reduces the chances for happiness: "Content and riches seldom meet together."

So you cut a deal with your able print shop foreman: he will take over running your business and pay you half his profits for eighteen years. Together with the income from your real estate holdings, that's enough for you to live on comfortably.

Okay, but what will you *do* with all this new spare time? Now that you have enough money to be a "gentleman" living off your investments, no longer a mere tradesman laboring with your hands, will you choose a life of upper-class idleness? You're so good at so many things, and the choices you've already made have brought you so far! But how can you make the most of the time you have left?

WHAT DO YOU DO, BEN? SELECT ONE:

A. Retire as a full-time gentleman.

Well, you do get a kick from the social upside of your growing success. America is lucky enough to have fewer extremes of wealth than England (where filthy-rich lords race carriages past starving peasants), but even the colonies have a class system, with a big gap between "gentlemen" and everyone else. Gentlemen typically are born rich, get elite educations, cultivate fine tastes, and work with their minds (if they feel like it) or not at all. Most other folk have no choice but to work, usually with their hands.

Congratulations! You're now a member of the upper class, and you've got too much ego not to flaunt it. As a gentleman, you recently had your portrait painted in a stiff pose. It shows you rocking a wig and expensive clothes, complete with ruffled sleeves. But surely there's more to life than living large?

B. Spend all your time writing.

You're Poor Richard, the man with the golden pen. Think how delighted your fans will be if you dedicate your days to giving them more of what they love! It would be a public service, really.

C. All science, all the time.

You are curious about *everything*, Ben. Lately, you've been particularly fascinated by the mysterious force known as electricity. From the moment you first saw static electricity demonstrated, in 1743, you've been tinkering with it on and off. You're making progress, but imagine what you could accomplish if you focus on electricity full-time. How cool would it be to unlock one of the greatest secrets in the universe?

D. Focus on politics.

You've shown how much you care about the public good, Ben, and it irks you to see the Penns getting away with their selfish shenanigans. They sure would hate if you get on their case full-time. (Heh, heh.) On top of that, you'd be helping the "middling people," and there could be no small glory in it for you. Sounds like win-win-win!

THE REVEAL

Y OU CHOSE . . . A. **Retire as a full-time gentleman.** "Gentleman" it is, but only because that's how you think you can accomplish the most good. Let's be clear: you have no desire to sit around all day doing nothing, like many retired gentlemen. You're just not cut out to do any *one* thing all day, every day. To you, being a gentleman means having time to do what's *useful*, even if it earns no money. You've always believed in making the most of your time: "Dost thou love life? Then do not squander time, for that's the stuff life is made of." You just want to free up your days from business for more important work—writing, science, *and* politics—while leaving room for a little fun on the side. So, in a way, you chose all of the above!

THE AFTERMATH

NOW, BEING A GENTLEMAN DOES have its lifestyle perks. No longer considering it fitting to live next to your print shop, you move to a different house. You send William to the best schools, raising him as a gentleman so he *never* has to work with his hands. You even acquire a coat of arms! Not bad for a poor boy from Boston.

Still, you never forget where you came from. For the rest of your life, you keep calling yourself a printer. You don't look down on hard work—far from it—but you do believe that those who don't *need* to work are in the best position to help society.

GENTLEMAN AUTHOR

OF COURSE, YOU DO CONTINUE writing. "Poor Richard" turns out almanacs for another ten years. A collection of his financial maxims, titled *The Way to Wealth,* will appear in 1757 and, over the next forty years, become a runaway bestseller in 145 editions and thirteen languages. You will go down in history as America's most popular humorist until maybe Mark Twain, whose style you will influence.

But for you, writing, like so many other things, is worthwhile mostly for the good you can *do* with it. You use it effectively in science, clearly explaining complex discoveries (see below), and especially in politics, winning arguments with a subtle mix of humor and logic. Despite a talent many authors would kill for, you would never consider writing full-time. You have fun with it, sure, but see it mostly as a tool for higher purposes.

GENTLEMAN EGGHEAD

YOUR NATURAL CURIOSITY WILL DRIVE you to experiment for the rest of your life, but you would never do *that* full-time, either. You believe serving country and community is more important than scientific research, if one has to choose—which, luckily, you don't.

You compile studies showing the value of smallpox immunization, for example, then write a preface for a pamphlet recommending it for all babies, then pay (out of your own pocket) to distribute fifteen hundred copies. Eventually, you will establish a society that immunizes the poor for free. Surely you will think of your darling son Franky, killed by smallpox, as you provide the funds. How many thousands of other children's lives will this generous and sentimental gesture end up saving?

What makes you the most famous scientist of the century, though, is your work with electricity. You capture it, you store it, you even use it to kill a turkey (almost frying yourself in the process). Scientists before you thought electricity was a kind of fluid, but *you* figure out that it's made up of two balancing forces, which changes everything. This is BIG! Your work creates a whole new field of science, and with it a new vocabulary: "positive and negative charges," "battery," "conductor," "grounding," and more.

You show that electricity is attracted to metal, particularly metal in the shape of a point. You guess that lightning, which people for millennia have assumed comes from divine fury, is really a form of electricity carried by the water droplets in thunderclouds. Then you prove it with (perhaps) the most famous experiment in science history: with William as your helper, you attach a bit of wire to a kite. You fly the kite in a raging storm, tie a key to the string's bottom end, and *draw sparks* from the key with your hand. Not only do you live to tell the tale, you even collect some of the lightning's energy in a battery to use for later.

Ben's kite experiment: not exactly how it happened.

Hundreds of people die every year when lightning hits buildings, with no shield to protect them other than prayer. So you invent the lightning rod, which (being metal, and pointed at the top) attracts the lightning and conducts it safely into the ground. Some cranky churchmen criticize your rods as offenses against God: if God wanted people to be safe, He wouldn't send lightning! But you point out that God seems to have no problem with roofs that protect against His hail and rain. Soon buildings all over America and Europe sprout lightning rods. The death rate from lightning strikes plummets, and your fame spreads around the globe.

Nice work, for a part-time scientist!

Gentleman Candidate

THIS FALL—IT'S 1748—YOU win a seat on the city council, where you soon push measures to improve Philadelphia's muddy, unsafe streets. You raise private and public funds to have them paved, then swept regularly, then lit. Being Ben Franklin, you even design a better streetlamp: it stays cleaner inside than the current British imports (smoke goes out a special vent on the bottom) and can be repaired more easily (its glass comes in four panes instead of the English globe).

You turn out to be a genius at fund-raising, along with everything else, twisting donors' and legislators' arms with a smile and a shrug of inevitability. Some people ask why you pay so much attention to small improvements such as paved streets, to which you reply, "Human [happiness] is produced not so much by great pieces of good fortune that seldom happen, as by little advantages that occur every day." True that.

UNITED COLONIES OF AMERICA?

THE CHALLENGE

NOW THAT YOU'RE A GENTLEMAN, you're getting to play with the big boys—which brings big challenges. How about this one: With a major war looming in America, can you turn thirteen ragtag colonies into a force to be reckoned with?

THE BACKSTORY

FOR A RETIREE, YOU'VE BEEN a busy guy. Your political career has progressed, and you now hold a seat in the Pennsylvania Assembly. Your election in 1751 forced you to give up your post as clerk, so you handed that job off to your son William, one of many times you'll help out your kinfolk with public positions.

You've continued to improve life for the citizens of Philadelphia, who until now have pretty much had to fend for themselves against problems like crime and illness. You've established a police force funded by taxes on property holders. You've promoted the creation of a hospital, beginning with an editorial in the *Gazette* and then (blazing new

DIDYA KNOW?

In Ben's day, physicians still "treated" many diseases by bleeding patients with leeches. Recently, though, leeches themselves have become medical heroes! Turns out their spit helps to prevent inflammation and clotting during surgery. Um . . . yay, leeches?

trails in fund-raising) getting the assembly to promise two thousand pounds *if* private citizens gave the same.

PENNSYLVANIA HOSPITAL

You've even established the Academy of Philadelphia (the future University of Pennsylvania) as America's fifth college and, importantly, its first college not linked to any one religion. Meanwhile, your astonishing discoveries about lightning have won you honorary degrees from Harvard and Yale. That makes you the only founder of one Ivy League college to get degrees from two others, all without ever attending *any* college!

Last year you even received a royal appointment: His Majesty's government made you co-head of the American postal service, allowing you to give William (of course) your Pennsylvania postmaster job. Needless to say, you're quickly improving the operation, introducing innovations such as home delivery (imagine not having to pick up your mail at the post office!) and super-speedy delivery (cutting the time it takes for letters to travel between Philadelphia and New York to only one day). Under your leadership the postal service will begin turning a big profit, some of which by right goes to you.

FUN FACT

The Ivy League also includes Princeton, Columbia, Brown, Cornell, and Dartmouth. The term (for colleges old enough to have ivy on the walls) was first used in the 1930s.

THE WRITE STUFF

NONE OF THIS, NATURALLY, STOPS you from writing. When the British insisted on shipping dangerous criminals to America (it was cheaper than jailing them), you penned a hilarious *Gazette* essay in protest, titling it "Rattlesnakes for Felons." Why not send a few thousand poisonous rattlesnakes to London, you proposed, in exchange for "the human serpents sent by our Mother Country"? The snakes could be let loose in the parks and *might* not hurt anyone. England would still get the better side of the trade, because "the rattlesnake gives warning before he attempts his mischief, which the convict does not."

On a more serious note, you wrote "Observations Concerning the Increase of Mankind, Peopling of Countries, etc." In this pioneering work, you made an incredibly accurate estimate of population growth in North America (doubling every twenty years, even without immigration). You explained that America's plentiful land allows its people to marry earlier and have more children, so the head count can grow much faster than in England; therefore, there will be more residents of America than of Britain by 1850. (Your theory of population expanding to use the available resources will influence later scientists such as Charles Darwin.) "Observations" also called it a mistake for England to outlaw American manufacturing (which it unfairly did to keep the colonies a captive market), because America's needs would soon outgrow the capacity of English factories.

You don't (yet) want to offend the powerful English, so neither of these pieces was published under your name, even though many people knew you wrote them. That tactful precaution has helped you gain not only the postal service job, but also an invitation to a prestigious conference in Albany, New York—which brings us to your next choice.

THE CHOICE

THE **ENGLISH HAVE ORGANIZED THIS** conference because their colonies have a problem, and once again the French and the Indians are involved. France has built a string of forts to the west, linking its territories in Canada (north) and Louisiana (south) and hemming in the British colonists near the coast. The Indians in the middle have to pick sides. Representatives of seven Northern colonies (Connecticut, Maryland, Massachusetts, New Hampshire, New York, Pennsylvania, and Rhode Island) are meeting with the Six Nations (Cayuga, Mohawk, Onondaga, Oneida, Seneca, and Tuscarora) in Albany to negotiate a treaty. After the Indians leave, the colonists will stay and discuss ways of working together against the French.

The English have never brought so many colonies together, because they prefer keeping them separate from one another and dependent on the "mother country." The colonies all have very different histories, cultures, even reasons for existing, and they don't really trust one another. Yet the French and Indian attacks threaten *all* of them. The colonies will do better by sticking together, but is cooperation even possible, given their history? As your writing shows (anonymously so far), unfair English moves like shipping over dangerous convicts and restricting American industry have made you increasingly distrust the mother country; how much can the colonies rely on the empire to protect them? Ben, you're always the man with a plan—but what *kind* of plan will you recommend for the colonies?

WHAT DO YOU DO, BEN? SELECT ONE:

A. Let every colony protect itself.

The colonies are so different from one another, and so far apart. Is it realistic to think they can rely on one another for help? Will Georgia send help if Indians invade New Hampshire, for example? Maybe it's best for each colony to stand on its own two feet. "God helps those who help themselves," you wrote in your almanac. If it works for people, why not for colonies?

B. Urge the colonies to unite.

As you showed in "Observations," you believe that the colonies have far more in common than otherwise. The go-it-alone strategy each colony has long been following is not working anymore: their lack of coordination has allowed France to make dangerous inroads to the west. "Observations" made clear that the colonies' growth depends on their freedom to expand westward, so being closed in by the French is an urgent problem.

You've already also proven that *colonists* can accomplish more (cleaner streets, fewer fire deaths, etc.) when they work together. Again, why not the same for *colonies*?

C. Propose whatever plan Pennsylvania wants.

John Penn, nephew of Thomas, is another delegate in Albany, but you and he do not exactly see eye to eye.

More and more, in fact, you resent the Penns' greedy ways and think they should (1) stop stealing land from the Indians and (2) pay their fair share of the colony's expenses. They don't seem to care about anyone but themselves! You still remember that when Thomas was living in Philadelphia, he ordered materials from your printing shop and never paid the bills. The amounts were small, which only makes his greed and arrogance stand out all the more.

But even if you don't feel like doing the Penns any favors, shouldn't you still want the best for Pennsylvania?

D. Tell the colonies to rebel.

Some colonists are starting to view the king a bit the way you see the Penns: more taking than giving. (King George is helping the Penns stay in power, in fact.) Increasingly, your fellow colonists are feeling like second-class citizens in the British Empire. Is it time to stop joking about rattlesnakes and strike for real?

THE REVEAL

YOU CHOSE . . . **B. Urge the colonies to unite.** You do want to help Pennsylvania, but you think teaming up with the other colonies is the best way to do that. In unity is strength.

THE AFTERMATH

THEY SAY A PICTURE IS worth a thousand words. To bolster your arguments, you publish a little drawing in the *Gazette* before heading north. Naturally (you *are* Ben Franklin), it becomes one of America's most famous political cartoons ever.

At the conference, you propose your Albany Plan of Union: a general council elected by the colonies, with a president general selected by the king. The general council would work together on common issues such as the French threat, while each colony kept power over its own internal affairs. If "six nations of ignorant savages" (you're not above using the period's bigoted language to make a point) can operate as a group, you argue, surely His Majesty's colonies can work together as well.

BTW, you're nowhere near ready to stir up rebellion. You still consider yourself English! You may disagree with some British policies, but you are confident that a reasoned discussion can sort out such differences among fellow countrymen.

That said, you do have a clear view of right and wrong. When someone suggests that the king (and not the colonists) should choose the general council, you object strongly: the general council could pay for defense by taxing the colonies, and "It is supposed an undoubted right of Englishmen not to be taxed but by their own consent given through their representatives." So you're against taxation without representation? Gee, that idea might catch on some day.

Meanwhile, your friend Thomas Hutchinson of Massachusetts helps your plan win approval by the other delegates. He's a calm and practical sort like you, raised in the same church, and only five years younger. Little could you imagine the role you will one day play in each other's lives!

Unfortunately, the colonies don't trust one another enough to accept the idea of *any* general council, no matter who elects it. Their assemblies all reject the Albany Plan, so your last hope is that Parliament (England's legislature) might still impose it from above. Think again: Parliament hates the idea too! In the House of Commons, the Speaker denounces "the ill consequences to be apprehended from uniting [the colonies] too closely," most of all the "independency from this country to be feared from such a union."

Ben, the problem with being a visionary is that other people can't yet see what *you* see. Without backing from England *or* the colonies, your Albany Plan never does become reality. If it had, history might have gone quite differently.

DEATH AND TAXES

THE CHALLENGE

THE NORTHERN COLONIES FAILED TO unite as you advised, so England had to send more troops to protect them. After defeating the French and their Indian allies, England has put an outrageous tax on the colonies—and you're caught in the middle. As you'll write, "In this world nothing can be said to be certain, except death and taxes." Can you handle *this* tax so it doesn't bring death in its wake?

THE BACKSTORY

THE COLONIES SUFFERED THROUGH THE French and Indian War from 1754 all the way into 1763. Because they rejected your Albany Plan, they badly needed the mother country to defend them. Protestant England was fighting a parallel war in Europe against Catholic France (and Spain), so it hardly relished the idea of sending troops across the Atlantic. Still, given the threat to its valuable American holdings, it had no other option.

When the British general Edward Braddock and his soldiers (called redcoats after their, uh, red coats) landed in 1755, you were among the Pennsylvanians sent to meet him. He had troops but not supplies, so you (being you) volunteered to help. In just two weeks, you rounded up enough horses and wagons for his entire army! Too bad you couldn't make him a better general: he underestimated the enemy and was killed in his first battle, with the immortal last words "Who would have thought it?"

I really expected that to go better.

The battle also devastated his army, including redcoats and local troops; one of the few surviving officers was a youngster named George Washington.

The Pennsylvania Assembly voted to raise a large sum for defense, but Thomas Penn's pet governor wouldn't let the Penn family be taxed for its share. This new outrage ruffled your usual calm: one official reported to Penn that your face "at times turns white as the driven snow with the extremes of wrath." You authored a furious reply from the assembly, saying that forcing the people to pay for defending the Penns' property (as well as their own) was an injustice "more slavish than slavery itself."

You then roused popular anger with the famous words "Those who would give up essential liberty to purchase a little temporary safety deserve neither liberty nor safety." This Franklin-led backlash forced the Penns to "volunteer" 10 percent of the total sum needed for defense.

DIDYA KNOW?

Braddock left Washington his ceremonial sash. For the rest of his life, Washington kept and often wore that sash—as rebel general, and even as president!

Money helped, but the colony needed soldiers, also. Guess who stepped in to raise a new militia and ended up being elected colonel of its Philadelphia regiment? You even served on the frontier for a couple of months. The Penns complained that the regiment escorted you around town with drawn swords, as if you "had been a member of the royal family or majesty itself." You didn't care what the Penn family thought: "The people happen to love me. Perhaps that's my fault."

Back to London!

OKAY, SO YOU NEVER CLAIMED modesty was your strong suit. But the assembly *did* love you enough to send you to London as their agent in 1757. Your mission: either get the Penns to see reason and treat the colony more fairly, or convince Parliament to save Pennsylvania from the founding family's greed.

After thirty years away, you were thrilled to be heading "home to England." You left your wife, Deborah, and daughter, Sally, in Philly but brought son William (age twenty-six) with you, settling into a comfortable London lifestyle that would last most of the next seventeen years. It didn't take you long to set up a kind of substitute household, renting rooms from the widow Margaret Stevenson and her daughter Polly. They were, let's be honest, a bit more refined than your own wife and daughter. You could bring them to parties, even discuss science with them—who could ask for more?

London, likewise, was even more your kind of town than Philly: way more sophisticated, over thirty times the size, and rich in scientists! Your famous experiments allowed you to join private clubs and befriend numerous politicians and intellectuals, hoping to enlist them as allies.

Thomas Penn, though, was not worried by your new connections: "There are very few of any consequence that have heard of his electrical experiments, those matters being attended to by a particular set of people. But it is quite a different sort of people who are to determine the dispute between us." Bad news: Penn was right. After you and he butted heads at a few unpleasant meetings, in which he stiff-armed all the assembly's demands (including that he pay his share of taxes), he refused to see you again.

Parliament was deaf to your pleas for justice, with

Penn's relationships outweighing yours. You weren't expecting the British government to be so dominated by the wealthy elite. Still, you blamed the Penns for your loss in Parliament, not the English.

DALLYING IN THE MOTHER COUNTRY

YOUR BUSINESS IN LONDON WAS essentially over within a year, but you were too stubborn to admit defeat and leave. Besides, you were having too much fun!

★ 1758: You studied evaporation with scientists in Cambridge; thanks to you, mankind learned that breezes cool people off through evaporation from their skin, not necessarily through colder air.

★ 1759: You spent the summer in Scotland, where you scooped up an honorary doctorate at the University of St. Andrews. From now on you're *Doctor* Franklin, thank you very much.

★ **1760:** Deborah's mom died in a kitchen fire. When she wrote you how lonely she was, you put her off by sending some gifts. (Another kind of husband might have sailed home to see her. Oh well.)

★ **1761:** You invented the "glass armonica," a musical instrument built from thirty-seven glass bowls of increasing size, which turned on a sideways axle. The player uses a foot pedal to spin the axle, touching different bowls with moistened fingers to bring forth otherworldly notes. The instrument will become a fad: Marie Antoinette will play it one day, and Beethoven and Mozart will admire it enough to compose for it.

The year 1761 also saw England crown a new king, the young George III. You have high hopes for him, trusting that he will take an enlightened view of the colonies and—who knows?—maybe even seize authority over Pennsylvania from its greedy proprietors, the Penns.

FUN FACT

A glass armonica later helped Franz Anton Mesmer to "mesmerize" patients and supposedly cure them. Ben himself, while in France, served on the commission that proved Mesmer was a quack!

WILLIAM: GOOD NEWS, BAD NEWS

BY 1762, YOUR CONNECTIONS IN government were good enough that William got appointed royal governor of New Jersey, really quite amazing for the illegitimate grandson of a Boston candlemaker.

William Temple Franklin (c. 1760-1823) Grandson of Benjamin Franklin. ~ Painted 1790-1823 ~

Check me out, coming up in the world!

Before leaving for his new post, William married rich in London, wedding Elizabeth Downes, daughter of a Barbados plantation owner. You should have been happy for William, but you didn't seem to like Elizabeth much or, for that matter, to feel as close to your son as you once had. You didn't approve of the aristocratic airs he started putting on after you brought him to London; could they have been the unintended result of your raising him as a gentleman? You were also perhaps a little jealous of his newfound government position, which you half advised him not to take.

There was another uncomfortable issue between you: William followed your example in 1760, fathering a son out of wedlock. He, unlike you, did not want to raise his son, farming him out instead to a foster family.

He didn't even acknowledge his baby with the Franklin name, calling him just William Temple (after the place in London where William was studying law). You did not approve. How much had changed between you since those happier times, when he was your eager student and lab assistant!

Significantly, you left England two weeks *before* William's London wedding, heading back to America at last to fulfill your postal duties. Your job there would soon cover more territory, because the war ended with England winning Canada from France and Florida from Spain. Surely you could have stayed until the wedding, though.

Finally Home—but Not for Long

ONCE HOME, YOU DIDN'T LINGER with Deborah in Philadelphia long but left on a seven-month tour to improve the postal system from New Hampshire to Virginia. Soon you sped up deliveries even more than before: a letter could travel from New York to Philly *and back,* all in less than a day—pretty amazing for 1763.

Not long after you finished your postal tour, a terrible

event occurred near Pennsylvania's frontier town of Paxton. A gang of settlers attacked and slaughtered about twenty local Conestoga tribe members, who were completely peaceful and innocent. Carried away with bloodlust, these "Paxton Boys" marched eastward, threatening to massacre any more Indians they could find, along with any softhearted Quakers who tried protecting them. You helped organize a force to fend off the mob, then wrote a heart-wrenching pamphlet that described the atrocity in gory detail. You named and described each of the "poor defenseless creatures" who were "inhumanly murdered." You called out the insanity of "white savages" who blamed harmless Indians for what other tribes had done, adding in capital letters, "THE BLOOD OF THE INNOCENT WILL CRY TO HEAVEN FOR VENGEANCE."

The new governor (Thomas Penn's nephew John) initially called the Paxton Boys criminals but, cynically grabbing a political opportunity, ended up siding with them and other anti-Quaker groups to organize a new anti-Franklin movement. Your popularity began to fall fast. Even some Quakers, led by the wealthy John Dickinson, rejected your latest big idea: to remove the Penns from their powerful role as proprietors and instead submit Pennsylvania to direct royal control (like most of the other colonies). Dickinson and his friends didn't like the Penns, but as Quakers they remembered that Pennsylvania *existed* because of royal anti-Quakerism. They saw your royalist proposal as a really, really bad idea. Facing all this new opposition, in 1764, you lost your assembly seat, though your supporters still kept a majority. Even worse, the Paxton Boys were not punished for their crimes.

Not so fast, Ben! Who wants to live in Georgesylvania?

Now you have crossed the Atlantic once more and are back in London, still acting as an agent for the assembly. You told Deborah you'd be gone a few months, but you hinted to others it might be years. In fact, you will be gone a decade, and you'll never again see your wife. You are rooming at the Stevensons', without William (off governing New Jersey) but with his son, William Temple, whom you'll keep with you from now on. You don't use the boy's first name at all, just calling him Temple.

THE CHOICE

PARLIAMENT, NEEDING TO PAY FOR the wars it just won against France and Spain, has decided to tax the Americans, given how much England spent (and is still spending) to protect them. The new Stamp Act requires colonists to buy a "tax stamp" for every newspaper, book, legal document, and even deck of cards they use. As an American, you dislike the idea of any tax; as a printer, you particularly object to a tax on printed goods.

The only piece of paper Ben didn't like.

You've told government ministers that this law would violate the British constitution, because Englishmen (as you consider the colonists to be) can't rightfully be taxed without the approval of their elected representatives. The ministers replied that the colonial assemblies were unlikely to pass taxes themselves, at least not to pay England (probably true).

Still, you can't believe Britain would be so short-sighted as to ruin its relationship with its most valuable colonies. You write to an English friend, "We are in your hands, as clay in the hands of the potter . . . as the potter cannot waste or spoil his clay without injuring himself, so I think there is scarce anything you can do that may be hurtful to us, but what will be as much or more so to you. This must be our chief security."

Your argument may make sense, but you have a dangerous blind spot: you sometimes assume other people will act sensibly, too. Parliament *has* foolishly passed the Stamp Act. Now you have to figure out how to spin the tax in your reports home. Should you ignore it, downplay it, denounce it, or go all the way and demand independence?

A. Ignore the Stamp Act.

Okay, this tax is kind of a big deal—the first-ever tax imposed directly on Americans by England. You know your fellow colonists will hate it; maybe that reaction will bring Parliament to its senses without *your* having to do anything. As you've told a Brit friend, "I wish some good angel would forever whisper in the ears of your great men, that dominion is founded in opinion." Wouldn't that be great?

B. Downplay the Stamp Act.

On the other hand, England thinks the colonists have been acting a bit entitled lately. Do they expect to get His Majesty's protection for *free*? If the colonies explode in anger at the tax, Parliament might take that as a challenge to its authority and refuse to back down. Perhaps a more measured American response would be more productive. And who better to cool things down than you, knowing both sides as you do? Maybe you should write home with some wise, moderate advice. Advice *is* one of your specialties, after all.

C. Denounce the Stamp Act.

You may be living in London, Ben, but you're not *from* there. The Stamp Tax is simply unfair to your fellow colonists. If you don't come out against it strongly, they might feel you've betrayed them. Didn't they send you across the ocean to represent their interests? And who in London is better suited than you to explain to Parliament just how inflammatory the tax will be? You might even get England to do the right thing and drop the tax.

D. Demand independence.

For many at home, the Stamp Tax will be the last straw. Anti-England sentiment has been growing for years now, and you could get ahead of that curve by calling for the colonies to liberate themselves. Maybe you should jump on the next ship to Philadelphia and help lead the fight for freedom from there! Not only would justice be on your side, but it could end up being a smart career move— if you win.

THE REVEAL

YOU CHOSE . . . **B. Downplay the Stamp Act.** Yikes! Sorry, Ben, but you've spent far too much time away from home. Foolishly, you imagine Americans will not take the tax so hard if some of them are appointed to collect it. You even recommend your friend John Hughes for that job in Pennsylvania! You also write home saying you tried to stop the tax, but "we might [as] well have hindered the sun's setting. That we could not do. But since it is down, my friend, and it may be long before it rises again, let us make as good a night of it as we can. We may still light candles."

THE AFTERMATH

SURPRISE: MANY AMERICANS ARE IN no mood to light candles—more like torches. In Massachusetts, they burn your friend Thomas Hutchinson's house to the ground (now lieutenant governor there, he had privately advised England *against* the tax). A congress of nine colonies meets in New York to deny that

Parliament has any right to tax them; ironically, they recycle your "Join, or Die" motto. Hutchinson writes you, "When you and I were at Albany ten years ago, we did not propose a union for purposes such as these."

As the colonies rise in protest, you keep up your tone-deaf letters: "Idleness and pride tax with a heavier hand than kings and parliaments. If we can get rid of the former, we can easily bear the latter." Yeah, right. Soon your name is hated in Pennsylvania, and anyone connected with you suffers. Your partners lose business, and your unfortunate friend Hughes (now tax collector) nearly loses his life. When a mob comes to burn down *your* house, brave Deborah has to stand guard with a few of your friends until help arrives.

BETTER LATE THAN NEVER

YOU SHOULD HAVE DENOUNCED THE tax right away. But once you realize your dreadful mistake, you go into heavy damage control mode. You write dozens of letters home, backed up by confirmations from London-based Quakers, declaring how firmly you opposed the tax. You write essay after (anonymous) essay for the London papers explaining what a mistake Parliament has made. You publish a rather gruesome cartoon showing the British Empire as a stout young lady unhappily dismembered, her limbs labeled with colony names; then you have it distributed outside Parliament. You  try to educate British decision-makers, "informing, explaining, consulting, disputing, in a continual hurry from morning to night."

What finally restores your reputation at home, though, is public testimony you give when called before Parliament as Pennsylvania's agent. You're generally a better writer than you are an orator, typically remaining silent even in the assembly. ("I was but a bad speaker, never eloquent, subject to much hesitation in my choice of words.") On this important day, though, you turn in a pitch-perfect performance. You answer 174 questions in all, scoring powerful points like these:

the colonies paid for most of their own defense, thank you; they don't need redcoats there anymore; they used to be "led by a thread" because of affection for England, but their love and respect are fading fast; armed enforcement of the tax simply will not work; an army sent to crack down "will not find a rebellion; they may indeed make one."

Soon afterward, Parliament repeals the Stamp Act. Huzzah! Georgia, then New Jersey, and eventually Massachusetts hire you as their agent in London, where you are now America's unofficial spokesman. Philadelphia names a barge after you, from which it fires salutes in your honor. All is (more or less) forgiven.

INDEPENDENCE? NO THANKS

N ANY CASE, BEN, YOU still have your own reasons not to push for independence. You are loyal to the mother country, and you hope that it might solve your Penn problem by taking over the colony. (The Penns actually outplayed you on the Stamp Act, refusing to nominate a collection officer because "the people might suppose we were consenting to the laying of this load upon them.")

The more you tangle with the Penns, the less you like them. Ever since your first bad boss (your big brother), nothing makes your blood boil like high-handed, unjust treatment. Your last meeting with Thomas Penn made you feel "a more . . . thorough contempt for him than I ever before felt for any man living." In this case you will ignore Poor Richard's wisdom: "Doing an injury puts you below your enemy; revenging one makes you but even with him; forgiving it sets you above him."

Ironically, the Stamp Act so destroys trust between Pennsylvanians and Parliament that it ends forever your dream of having the king take over the colony from the Penns. Unbeknownst to the assembly, though, you still have another big favor to ask of England, this one personal. You have your eye on land in the Ohio Country, the western territory that France handed over to England after the recent war. You've long had visions of America's westward expansion, and so you've begun suggesting that a major land grant be made to a group that you, conveniently, would lead. You will push this idea for years, actually coming pretty close to winning a significant grant as you enlist aristocratic partners. But then a new war will send the whole plan up in smoke.

A "SMALL LEAK"?

THE CHALLENGE

THE **STAMP ACT AND LATER** British actions helped bring the colonies to the brink of rebellion. Now you've been slipped a batch of secret letters that could push them over the edge. How do you treat information that's so sensitive, it might make the difference between war and peace?

THE BACKSTORY

YOU WERE RELIEVED WHEN **PARLIAMENT** finally repealed the Stamp Act—that is, until it passed *new* taxes the next year, 1767. To be fair, the so-called Townshend duties (import taxes on paper, glass, china, and other goods, including tea) were not direct taxes (paid directly by colonists). In your own testimony, you had told Parliament it would be okay to impose indirect taxes (such as duties, which consumers do not pay directly because they are hidden in the retail prices of goods). By 1767, though, Americans were so fed up with England that they rejected such fine distinctions. Protest groups had sprung up all over the colonies, including one in Massachusetts called the Sons of Liberty.

You again underestimated the reaction at home, though you weren't blindly pro-England, either. For one thing, you didn't like the way Parliament had begun referring to your countrymen as "our North American subjects." You're an Englishman! You're no one's "subject" but the king's, who you're hoping might have more affection for the colonies than does his arrogant, politically driven legislature.

You did your best to explain the Americans to the British and vice versa. You wrote letters home saying Americans should "hold fast [our] loyalty to our King (who has the best disposition towards us, and has a family interest in our prosperity)." Meanwhile, your essays in London papers warned that Americans should not be treated so shabbily. For instance, you wrote a nice parable of a dog who bullies a lion cub, then regrets it when the cub grows up (as America is now doing). But trying to keep *everyone* calm did not make you popular with *anyone*. You complained that people accused you "in England of being too much of an American, and in America of being too much of an Englishman."

Tensions mounted in 1770, when redcoats shot and killed protesters in Boston. This fateful event, the Boston Massacre, showed Parliament that revolution was becoming a real risk, so they repealed all the duties except those on tea. You warned them that would not be enough, but did they listen? They did not—and will wish they had.

Loving "At a Distance"

WITH ALL YOUR MANEUVERING IN London, you were too busy to travel home when Sally married shopkeeper Richard Bache in 1767, or when

FUN FACT

Paul Revere, soon to be famous for a certain "midnight ride," engraved this iconic picture of the Boston Massacre.

Deborah suffered a small stroke in 1769, which she blamed on her "dissatisfied distress" without you. Now she writes, "I find myself growing very feeble very fast," but still you do not go to see her.

You keep blaming your absence on duty, but now

that you've experienced London, how much would you really enjoying living in Philly with a woman who shares so few of your intellectual interests—who often signs letters "your a feck shonet wife"? You admit to your sister Jane that you may actually get along better with your family from far away, recalling your dad's opinion that "nothing was more common than for those who loved one another at a distance to find many causes of dislike when they came together." But you seem to get along fine with your London landlady and *her* family; Poor Richard may say that "fish and visitors stink in three days," but you and the Stevensons have seemed happy together for years.

Go home? In London, life is *good*. You have powerful friends. You get to dine with the visiting king of Denmark. The government cultivates you as a source of information and influence, even dangling before you a possible cabinet post (minister for the colonies, perhaps?). You can bask in the praise of your scientist friends when you recommend exercise as a cure for colds because it raises body temperature; when you diagnose lead poisoning in certain tradesmen, including typesetters; or when you demonstrate (with models) why ships move faster through deeper canals.

And when London feels too hot or dirty, you can travel to Scotland or France. You can visit the estate of rich Lord Shelburne, where you amaze your friends with a magic trick: smoothing out the ripples on a pond by pouring oil from a hidden compartment in your cane.

You can spend the whole summer at a wealthy bishop's country house, where you've begun work on the charming (though self-serving) book that will become the biggest-selling autobiography ever. You even ask Deborah to ship over an American squirrel as a pet for the bishop's kids. When their dog later kills poor Skugg, you console them with this epitaph:

Here Skugg
Lies snug
As a bug
In a rug.

Alas, poor Skugg!

In short, England offers you *so* much more opportunity for growth and fun than sleepy little Philadelphia. You will soon confess to Deborah that you fear "I shall find myself a stranger in my own country; and leaving so many friends here, it will seem leaving home to go there."

THE CHOICE

NOW, THOUGH, NEWS FROM AMERICA is demanding your attention. Someone has slipped you hush-hush letters from your old friend

Thomas Hutchinson to a British minister. He wrote them a few years ago, when he was still lieutenant governor of Massachusetts, but now he is governor. You can tell immediately that these letters are hot, hot, hot: Hutchinson was warning his British overlords that the colonists were getting too uppity, too greedy for more rights. To keep the peace, he advised, "There must be an abridgment of what are called English liberties." Clearly, he was telling London to crack down—to ignore Americans' civil rights. And England *did* crack down soon after, producing the Boston Massacre. Could Hutchinson thus be partly to blame for the massacre and for the wildfire of unrest since then? But . . . but he's an American!

If published in America, Hutchinson's letters would be like dynamite. They could raise enough explosive questions to set off a revolution: Was the Boston Massacre part of some plot against the colonies? If so, was Hutchinson behind it, or the English, or both? Is there *anyone* Americans can trust? Now that the letters have fallen into your lap, though, the first question you need to decide is this: What in heaven's name do you do with them?

A. Burn the letters.

This would be the honorable thing to do. Hutchinson is a decent man, a pragmatist after your own heart, who (like you) seems to be trying to prevent war. He had the right ideas in Albany, he warned against passing the Stamp Act, and he generally has good sense. He was also, by the way, extremely helpful to your sister Jane after her husband died. Is there anything wrong with his holding a British imperial post? After all, you do, too. Maybe Hutchinson's advice in the letters was misguided, but he meant well. His private correspondence should be nobody's business but his.

Back in the 1720s, when you were writing as Busy-Body for Bradford's *Mercury*, you joked that "out of zeal for the public good" you would "take nobody's business into my own hands." You *were* joking, right?

B. Keep the letters.

Might be wise. If you aren't going to burn the letters, at least you can keep them safe, knowing how inflammatory they could be. That way, you'll still have them if for some reason you need them later.

C. Leak the letters.

The people have a right to know—don't they? If nothing else, you would prove Poor Richard right: "Three may keep a secret if two of them are dead."

D. Publish the letters.

You *are* a publisher, right? Someone who believes in printing the truth for all to read? You did sort of promise, when you got the letters originally, not to publish them. But maybe you can do it anonymously, or using some other name (and not something obvious like Neb Nilknarf).

Wouldn't be a big leap for you, Ben. You've been writing under assumed names (Silence Dogood, Busy-Body, Richard Saunders, and dozens of others) your whole life. During your time in England, you will end up publishing about ninety items under forty-two (yes, forty-two) different pseudonyms. Pen names can serve legitimate purposes: you can present arguments on their own merits, escape censorship, and encourage people who personally dislike you to read with open

minds. But false bylines can also have less honorable purposes, like avoiding lawsuits or the need for consistency.
In any case, though, *these* letters are so hot that publishing them anonymously might not protect you.

THE REVEAL

YOU CHOSE . . . **C. Leak the letters.** It pains us to
say this, but you leak. Is it right? No, but you persuade yourself it is.

You're good at persuading yourself of things, Ben—
maybe too good. Your autobiography tells how you once
decided to be a vegetarian, and you stuck to it—until,
when you were fleeing Boston by ship, the crew caught
some cod. The fish smelled so good, frying there on
deck! You resisted the temptation for a while but then
remembered seeing smaller fish inside the cod's stom-
achs when they were cut open. "Then, thought I, 'If you
eat one another I don't see why we may not eat you;' so
I dined upon cod very heartily, and have since continued to eat as other people." The moral? "So convenient

a thing it is to be a reasonable creature, since it enables
one to find or make a reason for everything one has a
mind to do."

THE AFTERMATH

YOU IMAGINE THAT BLAMING HUTCHINSON will
make Americans feel better about England
somehow ignoring that England, after all, *took*
Hutchinson's advice. A genius you may be, Ben, but
you have just made a really, really stupid mistake. In
your own words, "A small leak will sink a great ship."

You should have just kept the letters. It's so disappoint-
ing, Ben, that you of all people missed this logical choice.
After all, you are the guy who has already invented the
world's most elaborate system for making tough decisions. You call it moral algebra, and you use it to prevent
a common mistake in decision-making, namely giving too much weight to whatever considerations have
occurred to you most recently. "To get over this, my way
is to divide half a sheet of paper by line into two columns;
writing over the one Pro, and over the other Con." Then
you take three or four days to write down all the reasons

that present themselves, for or against. Finally, you cross out any pros and cons that seem to balance each other out, until the "weight" of the reasons is clearly on one side or the other. Moral algebra may take longer, but it's usually worth the extra care—for you.

But one of your weaknesses as a politician is that you, with all your reasoned analysis, do not understand how very different most folks are from you. You continually underestimate the speed and force of regular people's emotions. "Every affront is not worth a duel," you write, "every injury not worth a war . . . every mistake in government, every encroachment on rights is not worth a rebellion." True enough, but where to draw the line? Not everyone stops to work out pros and cons the way you do.

FIRESTORM!

YOU'RE NOT RECKLESS ENOUGH TO publish the letters yourself, but you do send them to a friend in Massachusetts, telling him to keep them quiet (uh-huh) but show them to "some men of worth in the province." Your cover letter (wrongly) accuses Hutchinson of "bartering away the liberties of [his] native country for posts, and negotiating for salaries and pensions, for which the money is to be squeezed from the people . . . creating enmities among the countries of which the empire consists." (Notice how you're calling America a country?) You call Hutchinson a betrayer of both England and America. If he *really* wants peace, you say, then he shouldn't object to having his wicked advice exposed, because then the colonists will know to blame him and not the king for "most if not all our present grievances."

So others publish them instead, throughout Massachusetts. That colony goes into turmoil, with its assembly demanding that England fire Hutchinson immediately. (He will cling to office until 1774, then spend the last six years of his life in bitter English exile.) You foolishly tell your British friends, now that the colonists have a scapegoat in Hutchinson, "their resentment against England is thence much abated."

You wish! In reality, the Sons of Liberty see the letters as evidence of a conspiracy *between* Hutchinson and the British, which they've been suspecting for years. When the assembly reacts by declaring it is not subservient to Parliament at all, you tell the powers that be not to worry: "It is words only." Oh, Ben.

Worst of all for you, your role in this fiasco inevitably comes to light. After two men fight a duel in London

because one accused the other of leaking the letters, you feel you must step forward (ironically) to prevent further bloodshed. Say goodbye to your reputation for honor, which means so much to you! It won't be long before the Hutchinson letters make you one of the most hated men in England.

"THERE NEVER WAS A GOOD WAR OR A BAD PEACE"

THE CHALLENGE

AFTER GETTING ROASTED BY THE British press and Parliament for the Hutchinson leak, you've finally left London. As you return to America, how can you prevent the unrest there from exploding into a full-scale revolution? Do you even want to?

THE BACKSTORY

YOU SPENT MUCH OF 1773, before the Hutchinson affair blew up, trying with clever satires to explain American gripes to the English. Two of these pieces provoked the most reaction:

★ "An Edict by the King of Prussia" states officially that the English include many people of Germanic heritage, so Prussia now intends to treat them as its own lowly "colonists": restrain their trade, shut their factories, burden them with Prussian convicts, and so on. Many British readers were outraged by Prussia's audacity—until they realized that England was already doing similar things to the Americans, so this "edict" was really a prank with a point.

★ "Rules by Which a Great Empire May Be Reduced to a Small One" helpfully lists twenty tips for any country wishing to shrink its "extensive dominions, which from their very greatness are become troublesome

to govern." Not coincidentally, all twenty
are measures that England has used or is
considering using against America: sending bad
governors, ignoring petitions, levying heavy
taxes, refusing representation, and so forth.
The clear warning: England is doing everything
wrong if it wants to *keep* the colonies.

You sent copies of both pieces to your sister Jane, saying you "have held up a looking-glass by which some ministers may see their ugly faces, and the nation its injustice." Why the extra-sharp satire? "I grew tired of meekness when I saw it without effect. . . . *If you make yourself a sheep, the wolves will eat you.*"

The wolves started licking their chops in December 1773, though, when you confessed to leaking the Hutchinson letters. You tried to justify your sneakiness, claiming you had only promised not to *publish* the letters, which you never (personally) did. You said it was all Hutchinson's fault for trying to "incense the Mother Country against her colonies," but no one listened. Your good name in England was lost, and the press filled with insults and tirades such as the following:

> *Thou base, ungrateful, cunning,*
>   *upstart thing!*
> *False to thy country first, then to*
>   *thy King,*
> *To gain thy selfish and ambitious ends,*
> *Betraying secret letters writ to friends.*

NOT THEIR CUP OF TEA

AN EVEN BIGGER EVENT THAT month dealt a further blow to your reputation *and* your efforts to improve colonial relations. The Sons of Liberty, in a dramatic burglary, dumped hundreds of cases of British tea into Boston Harbor. You were shocked by this "act of violent injustice on our part," but the English blamed *you* for inciting the vandalism.

In January 1774, the king's ministers hauled you into a public chamber called the Cockpit (it once hosted cockfights) for a piece of political theater. There, courtiers and officials listened, chortling and cheering, while England's chief lawyer humiliated you for over an hour. You might *pretend* to be a gentleman, he jeered, but you were really just a common thief who had "forfeited all the respect of societies and of men." He even turned your achievements against you, sniggering that you were a "man of letters" (nudge, nudge) and the "inventor" and "prime conductor" (wink, wink) of American unrest. The day after this public shaming, you got fired from your prized job at the postal service.

So you left London with your tail between your legs, right? No, you did not. During that whole hour in the Cockpit, you made a point of standing erect and expressionless in your blue velvet suit, and you kept your cool afterward as well. Bravo, but why stay in town? Because, despite all the terrible things that have happened, you still think there's a chance for peace.

Scandalized by the Boston Tea Party (which won't be called that for about fifty years), you offered to pay for the tea out of your own pocket. Nice try: the Brits are now standing on the principle of respect for the law.

Over the next year, you discussed top-secret peace terms with politicians including a former prime minister—but when he proposed them publicly, Parliament's House of Lords shouted him down without even a vote. The other lords suspected your part in this last-ditch attempt at peace; one spotted you in the gallery and called you "one of the bitterest and most mischievous enemies this country has ever known."

Finally, when a member called Americans "the lowest of Mankind and almost a different species from the English of Britain," you realized that Parliament was beyond hope. You wrote that it had barely enough wisdom "to govern a herd of swine" and made plans to return to America.

Hey, Parliament, bring it on!

You left in March 1775. Seldom have you been more frustrated at other people's irrationality. Joseph Priestley, a scientist friend with whom you shared your last day in England, later recalled that you were (for you) quite upset: as you read aloud from the newspaper about the fast-mounting chance of war between the two lands you loved, you had to stop—because of the tears in your eyes.

You've spent the voyage home in typical Franklin fashion: charting a weirdly warm ocean current and naming it the Gulf Stream. You may be a sixty-nine-year-old grandpa, but you're still curious about everything in this world. With help from your

> ## FUN FACT
>
> The Gulf Stream is actually part of the North Atlantic Gyre, which flows clockwise. South of the equator, gyres rotate counterclockwise, as do most hurricanes (but not toilet flushes—that's just a myth).

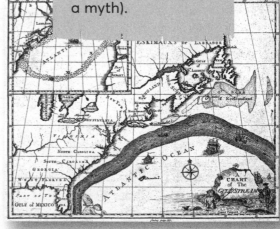

grandson Temple, whom you're bringing home, you've tracked the ocean's temperature several times a day. From this carefully gathered data you will develop maps of the Gulf Stream that future scientists will, one day, find remarkably accurate.

THE CHOICE

NOW, THOUGH, YOUR SHIP IS approaching Philadelphia. It's time to decide what you'll tell your fellow Americans. Will you keep advocating for peace, which you love so much, or will you come out for independence? And, if you can't decide yet, will you keep busy by focusing on your family, from whom you've been away so long, or perhaps on the affairs of Pennsylvania?

WHAT DO YOU DO, BEN? SELECT ONE:

A. Push for independence.

When your ship reaches shore, Philadelphia bells ring in celebration: here, at least, the Hutchinson letters have made you a hero again. Reporters meet you on the dock, asking for your outlook on the country you just left. Can we all just get along?

Here are some good reasons to just say no. First, you're a realist: Shouldn't you finally accept that peace is a lost cause for now? Feelings (the enemies of your beloved logic) are just too strong on both sides. Second, since war seems unavoidable anyway, you might as well squash any rumors that you are still "too much of an Englishman" to be a patriotic American. Third, you truly are seething at the unjust and arrogant way England is treating America. Finally, you yourself feel insulted and mistreated by the English, and bullies have *always* made you see red.

B. Argue for peace.

Hey, you just got off the ship. You don't know yet about the Battles of Lexington and Concord, the famous "shot heard round the world," which happened during your voyage. And you're no fan of warfare: you often say things like "There never was a good war or a bad peace." Why give up the fight for peace now?

C. Concentrate on Pennsylvania.

Pennsylvania's been good to you, Ben. And it was primarily Pennsylvania you were sent overseas to represent.

You've been away so long. Why not focus on your home turf, and let the other colonies take care of themselves?

D. Focus on your family.

Ah, family. What could be more important, right?

And your family relations badly need attention, especially William. After getting humiliated in the Cockpit and fired from the royal postal service, you pressured him to resign as governor of New Jersey. You suggested farming: "It is an honester and more honorable, because more independent, employment." But maybe the real reason you thought he should resign was out of loyalty to you, whom England had treated so badly?

In any case, William's loyalty lay elsewhere; he felt he should stay and faithfully serve his king. His royalist attitude clearly bothered you. When William wrote that Boston should pay for the dumped tea, you replied, "But you, who are a thorough courtier, see everything with government eyes." Pretty harsh, given that you, too, felt the Tea Party was wrong.

Then you kept postponing your return from London until after Deborah died. "Honored father, I came here on Thursday last," William wrote from Philadelphia the day before Christmas 1774, "to attend the funeral of my poor old mother, who died Monday . . . I heartily wish you had happened to come over in the fall, as I think her disappointment in that respect preyed a good deal on her spirits."

Now that you're home at last, maybe you should focus on William and your faithful daughter, Sally. You're the only dad they've got, Ben.

THE REVEAL

YOU CHOSE . . . A. Push for independence. It's finally time! There on the dock, you pull no punches: "We have no favors to expect from the ministry; nothing but submission will satisfy them." Only a "spirited opposition" will save America from "the most abject slavery and destruction."

THE AFTERMATH

NOW THAT YOU'VE DECIDED, YOU go all in. The day after landing, you agree to join the new Continental Congress (which has representatives from all thirteen colonies) as its oldest member. There you mostly sit quietly, as is your habit, but eventually you stand out as one of the most radical delegates. According to John Adams, a Massachusetts revolutionary, "He does not hesitate at our boldest measures, but rather seems to think us too irresolute." In July you even submit to the Congress a draft agreement you call Articles of Confederation and Perpetual Union, which is like your Albany Plan—but with no king. You're so far ahead in your thinking that the Articles will not get serious consideration for another year.

Not all the delegates even favor independence at first. For example, your enemy John Dickinson persuades the Continental Congress to send a message, the Olive Branch Petition, directly to the king. It basically begs him to avert a war they blame on his "irksome" and deluded ministers. George III will pretty much grab this olive branch, snap it in two, and whittle arrows from it: he'll not only reject the petition but declare "his" colonies in revolt.

LETTER BY LETTER

YOU SEE IT COMING. ON the same day that the Congress passes the petition, you make public this letter to one of your dearest friends in England:

You are a Member of Parliament, and part of that majority which has doomed my country to destruction. You have begun to burn our towns, and murder our people. Look upon your hands! They are stained with the blood of your relations! You and I were long friends. You are now my enemy, and

I am,

Yours,

B. Franklin

You never actually send this famous letter; it was written for American readers. You keep many of your British friends, although those letters you *do* send to them show a new edge. To Mrs. Stevenson you send back rent, with advice not to invest it in English companies: "Britain having begun a war with us, which I apprehend is not soon to be ended, there is great probability of these stocks falling headlong."

To scientist Joseph Priestley you offer this war math: "Britain, at the expense of three million [pounds], has killed 150 Yankees this campaign, which is £20,000 a head . . . During the same time, 60,000 children have been born in America. From these data [a] mathematical head will easily calculate the time and expense necessary to kill us all." FYI, three million pounds is equivalent to almost $1 billion in 2019 dollars.

You make clear to Priestley whose fault the war is: "In my conscience I believe that mankind are wicked enough to continue slaughtering one another as long as they can find money to pay the butchers. But of all the wars in my time, this on the part of England appears to me the wickedest, having no cause but malice against liberty and the jealousy of commerce."

Say what you really think, Ben.

JOSEPH PRIESTLEY,
B. 1733—d. 1804 A. D.

Another letter, though, shows how you love your friends even if you hate their rulers. Your harshest criticism ("Do you think it prudent by your barbarities to fix us in a rooted hatred of your nation, and make all our innumerable posterity detest you?") is closely followed by hopes that "your dear little girl is well, and that you continue happy."

A Revolutionary PR Genius

I N LATE 1775, YOU SPOT a rattlesnake painted by a marine drummer on the side of his drum, with the words "Don't Tread on Me." You publish an essay proposing that the symbol be widely adopted, because the rattlesnake, an American species, never starts a fight but never runs away from one. (This is your *third* snake piece, after "Join, or Die" and "Rattlesnakes for Felons." Interesting.) The Congress agrees, and soon the marines and many militia units fly "Don't Tread on Me" flags.

In November, you publish "The King's Own Regulars," a mocking song from the redcoats' perspective, telling how they ran away at Lexington when the

Americans started shooting. The ditty's a hit, with a last verse that goes, "As they could not get before us, how could they look us in the face? / We took care they shouldn't, by scampering away apace. / That they had not much to brag of, is a very plain case; / for if they beat us in the fight, we beat them in the race." So now you're a songwriter, too?

In January 1776, you help Thomas Paine, a Quaker you met in London, to publish his pamphlet "Common Sense." It soon sells more than a hundred thousand copies, and its antiroyalty passion raises revolutionary feelings to fever pitch. There is "no natural or religious reason for the distinction of men into kings and subjects," insists Paine. "Of more worth is one honest man to society and in the sight of God than all the crowned ruffians that ever lived." At first, many folks take the words for yours.

Is that all I am to you, George? A sore subject?

MAKING IT OFFICIAL

IVEN ALL THIS, IT'S ONLY natural that the Continental Congress should include you in its committee to draft the Declaration of Independence. Thomas Jefferson becomes chairman, partly because he's from Virginia, the most populous colony. John Adams asks him to write the first draft, admitting that he himself is "obnoxious, suspected, and unpopular" within the Congress and that Jefferson "can write ten times better than I can." You suggest many edits, including this important one: where Jefferson tries, "We hold these truths to be sacred and undeniable" (that all men are created equal, etc.), you change it to the more persuasive, "We hold these truths to be self-evident." Written like a true scientist!

Fine. "Self-evident." Whatever.

When the Congress finally votes on the Declaration, your own Pennsylvania delegation won't support it until you manage to bring them in line through your powers of persuasion, and the motion passes. Even then, your old enemy Dickinson, the Quaker who cost you your assembly seat back in 1764, resists all your coaxing and ends up abstaining. How much does he hate you? This much: he still refuses to put a lightning rod on his house, though that means risking death by fire.

As president of the Congress, John Hancock puts his big signature on the document. A famous story has him warning, "There must be no pulling different ways. We must all hang together," to which you agree, "Yes, we must, indeed, all hang together, or most assuredly we shall all hang separately." A little black humor there: if England wins, whoever signs this document is likely to face the gallows for treason. Declaring independence is risky business!

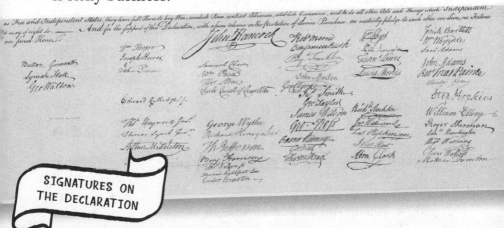

SIGNATURES ON
THE DECLARATION

Even after the Declaration, you are willing to hear peace proposals, for all the good it does. Richard Howe, the commanding British admiral, sends you a letter in July 1776 offering to accept the Olive Branch Petition after all, with pardons for the Continental Congress. (He knows you from London, where he actually worked with you for peace, and he can't officially recognize the Congress by sending *them* a letter.) You read the letter to the Congress and draft a reply saying sorry, too late: there can now be no peace without independence.

Howe still requests a face-to-face, so you and he meet up in Staten Island, New York. John Adams travels with you; you two have to share a room on the way and end up fighting over whether to keep the window open. He says no—he has a cold. You say yes and back it up with so many medical arguments for fresh air that Adams gives in, which almost never happens. You do not catch his cold.

The meeting is friendly but useless: the two sides have long been too far apart for peace. The British have just captured Long Island (nearly trapping Washington and his troops in Brooklyn) and now, following the failed peace talks, proceed to seize New York City. The war has begun in earnest, and nothing will end it but defeat or, possibly, victory.

Your Favorite ~~Colony~~ State

MEANWHILE, YOU DO MAKE *SOME* time for Pennsylvania matters; for example, after signing the Declaration, you serve as president of the new state's own constitutional convention. You persuade the delegates there to create only one legislative house because you believe two would be less effective. (You carry the point with a Franklinesque parable about a snake born with two heads—again with the snakes! The snake can't decide which of two ways to slither toward a nearby stream and so dies of thirst.) You also persuade them not to require state office holders to be men of property, which to you seems undemocratic.

More than most Americans, though, you see yourself as a citizen of the whole country, and your country needs you. (Remember, you started pushing for American unity in 1754!) You are constantly finding new ways to serve the nation. You're entrusted with the new job of postmaster general; you donate your whole salary to the war cause (but appoint your son-in-law to administer the department's finances); you help design the nation's new currency and the Great Seal (with the words *"E Pluribus Unum"*—"from many, one"); you supervise the collection of lead for ammunition; you oversee the making of gunpowder; you lead a congressional tour of the army in Massachusetts; you even brave a winter trek to Canada, trying in vain to convince its citizens to join in rebellion against England. (On the way, you buy a fur cap that will soon come in handy on a very different trip.)

You help create the relatively loose Articles of Confederation in the summer of 1776. Even now, the states do not trust one another enough to accept your idea of a stronger central government. That will have to wait for the US Constitution, eleven years hence.

Thanks a Lot, Dad

BUT WHAT ABOUT YOUR FAMILY? In that respect, your homecoming left something to be desired: William learned about it in the paper as "quite unexpected news to me." You couldn't give him a heads-up?

You meet your son at a friend's house, where each of you tries to change the other's politics. Good luck with that. You tell William that America must have its freedom, while he worries for your safety if you persist: if you do "set the colonies in flame," then you should "take care to run away by the light of it." Neither side budges, and that is the last time you will see each other for ten years.

It's really a tragedy, Ben. You've poured so much love and attention on your only living son, raising him as a "gentleman" with all the advantages you never had. Yet in doing so, you've created a person who saddens you: entitled where you preach frugality, pompous where you love humor, averse to political change where you seek social justice, English at heart where you're American. He often tries to do the right thing and loves you in his own way, but your lower-class roots embarrass him. So he's taken after you in the most painful way: declaring independence from his own father. To William, *you're* the authority figure to reject.

Each step he's taken to become his own man has wounded your feelings, causing you to withdraw inch by inch yourself. After years of growing distance, you're each too bitter, too angry, too far apart, to bridge the gap. You've lost each other. It's a heartrending dynamic—and sadly similar to the chasm between the colonies and their "mother country," England.

So you do not help William when the rebels start arresting royal governors. His wife, Elizabeth (scared, alone, surrounded by "unruly soldiers"), begs you to have him released on parole, which you could probably do, but you refuse and won't even visit before she dies, in 1777. Still defiant (where does he get that from?), William later gets exiled to England, never to return.

At least Sally has never rejected you. You're fond of her, and especially of her bright eldest child, whom she has endearingly named Benjamin Franklin Bache. You take "Benny" and Temple with you on your next and greatest adventure: America is sending you to France! It's the one country that can help America win its freedom. Your nation needs you, because no other American has the fame and prestige in France that you do. Although you tell the Continental Congress you'd rather not go, you hint otherwise: "I am old and good for nothing. But as the storekeepers say of their remnants of cloth . . . you may have me for what you are pleased to give."

The fact is, you are eager for this mission, for which you are uniquely suited. October 27, 1776: you sail for France on the USS *Reprisal.*

CELEBRITY, SECRETS, AND SPIES

THE CHALLENGE

AFTER HELPING **AMERICA TAKE ITS** first real steps toward independence, you've become the new country's top agent in Europe. But how can you help your homeland win its freedom from England when someone keeps leaking all your secrets to London?

THE BACKSTORY

BEN, REMEMBER THOSE FIGHTS YOU had with James when you were seventeen? Remember how unfair he was, how controlling, how cruel when he beat you? Luckily, there was nothing he could do to stop you from running away, and your apprenticeship would have ended in a few years anyway. But now England is acting worse than James ever did: it's using brutal violence so as to keep America in bondage—forever.

Imagine if James *had* tried harder to keep you under his thumb, beating you bloody and threatening worse. Without the law on your side, would you have been desperate enough to turn to an old enemy for help? Suppose the Franklins had a longstanding feud with another guy—call him Pierre. Say this Pierre was totally alien to your family: different language, different religion, different background altogether—and, by the way, cruel to his own younger brothers. But what if Pierre was almost as strong as James, and really hated James? Would you have asked Pierre for help, not knowing if he'd say yes, what price he'd demand, or even if you could trust him?

Okay. If you're America in this scenario, and James is

England, then Pierre is France. And the situation really is that bizarre. France is Catholic, it's been deadly foes with England and its colonies for centuries, and America is rebelling mostly over English taxes arising from a just-finished war against . . . France! Not only that, but France's Louis XVI allows his subjects even less freedom than George III permits. If *French* rebels shouted "Give me liberty or give me death!" like your American friends, guess which one Louis would give them?

With Enemies Like This, You Need France

AND YET HERE YOU ARE in Paris. Why? Desperation. When you arrived in Paris, you'd just cosigned a declaration that poked the world's mightiest empire in the eye. Now it's 1778, and England's navy still "rules the waves," as its song goes. The British army is no slouch, either, having recently won a major war on two continents (actually, three: it beat the French in India at the same time). The newborn America has almost no navy, and its Continental "army" is tiny, with no uniforms, weapons, or funding to speak of. Without major assistance, your new nation is clearly doomed.

That explains why you came to France: for money, arms, soldiers, *help*. But why has France received you so warmly, and why might it agree to become America's new best friend? After all, France and its Catholic ally Spain have just been trounced by England; why take on a new, uncertain war? France has other options, for sure. It could cut a deal with England, staying out of the war in exchange for North American territory, or it could follow Spain's idea of providing only a *little* help. Spain worries that an independent America might one day pose a threat in the New World but is happy to send over just enough aid to weaken Britain.

Lucky for you, France is convinced that America will never be a threat, because England's Canadian presence will continue to limit the new nation's strength and ambition. France holds a serious grudge against England and wants access to American trade, tobacco in particular. But a major reason why France may tip the Revolutionary War in America's favor is one amazing diplomat, perhaps the best the States will ever produce: you.

BEN, *LE ROCKSTAR!*

YOU WERE A CELEBRITY EVEN before you arrived. France's elite are proud that its scientists were the first to replicate your experiments with electricity, and your writings are bestsellers here, especially *The Way to Wealth* (translated as *La science du bonhomme Richard*). When you reached Paris, throngs lined the streets just hoping for a glimpse of your wise face—a face that soon appeared on mugs, rings, medals, dishes, etchings, portrait busts, and all manner of other knickknacks.

You soon wrote to Sally, pretending to be embarrassed, "The numbers sold are incredible. [They] have made your father's face as well known as that of the moon."

French intellectuals admire you as a scientist: they're in love with "reason"—with wisdom tested by logic and knowledge gained by experiment—thanks to Enlightenment philosophers such as Voltaire and Rousseau. They also thrill to your passion for liberty; it doesn't hurt that the British papers slammed you before you left London as "chief of the rebels." But what they really adore is your plain *American*-ness. To them, you (a city boy!) embody the pioneer spirit, the land of fresh beginnings, the adventure of the New World.

For example: the French go gaga over that fur cap you picked up on your recent trip to Canada. Many portraits show you in it, and women have even begun wearing their hair *à la Franklin,* woven to look like that frontier cap. Your legions of French fans consider you a true man of

D: Benjamin Franklin.

nature—ironic, given that you've lived in cities your whole life, but you'll take popularity any way it can help America.

It actually helps that you don't talk much here (partly because your French is only so-so). The French just rave about your "simplicity and innocence" and "unalterable serenity." Whatever works, right?

England knew you'd be dangerous. London filled with rumors that you, the brilliant scientist, were conniving with the French to attack England with diabolical new weapons, maybe giant mirrors (to torch the British fleet) or huge electric shocks (to start earthquakes). Lord Stormont, Britain's shrewd ambassador to France, thought you could do plenty of damage *without* your technology: "As [Franklin] is a subtle,

I'm watching you, Ben.

artful man, and void of all truth, he will in [the rebel] cause use every means to deceive, will avail himself of the general ignorance of the French to paint the situation of the rebels in the falsest colors, and hold out every lure to the ministers to draw them into an open support of that cause." Not that you respect *his* honesty much yourself, often saying, "It is not a truth; it is only a Stormont." You've even coined a new French word: *stormonter,* "to lie."

FRIENDS IN NEED

YOU'VE GOT HELP IN YOUR mission from a motley band of Frenchmen, these four in particular:

★ The Marquis de Lafayette: one of the richest men in France, though only twenty-one years old. His father was killed fighting the British, so his main reason to help you is revenge: "To injure England is to serve my country." Last year, in 1777, he sailed for America on his own ship, with a letter of introduction from you. He will play a major role in key battles, return as a hero, and help you get gigantic loans for America from his king.

★ **Pierre de Beaumarchais:** playwright, watchmaker, musician, adventurer, and financier. He was first to hop on the American bandwagon, convincing King Louis to start sending money even before you declared independence. He's also arranged the first shipment of uniforms and muskets, which are proving vital to Washington's early victories. Beaumarchais is in it for the love of liberty; his plays, such as *The Barber of Seville* and *The Marriage of Figaro*, champion the common man against haughty nobles. But he offers economic reasons to Louis, claiming that every franc spent for America will bring eight back to France and cost England a hundred. And he doesn't mind turning a profit himself, whether from shipping supplies or from using his inside war info to trade stocks.

★ **The Comte de Vergennes:** Foreign minister who hates the British. He writes things to Louis such as "England is the natural enemy of France; and she is an avid <u>enemy</u>, ambitious, unjust, brimming with bad faith; the permanent and cherished object of her policy is the humiliation and ruin of France." He may be willing to help America, though so far only unofficially: "One can connive at certain things, but one cannot authorize them." And he tells Stormont not to worry that you keep visiting: "A minister's residence is like a church. Anyone can enter, although there is no guarantee he will be absolved."

FUN FACT

Vergennes previously served as French ambassador to the Ottoman Empire. He didn't dress like this in Paris!

★ **Jacques de Chaumont:** rich, noble, well connected at court. He's providing you with a free, fully staffed mansion in the leafy suburb of Passy, perfectly situated between Paris and the royal court at Versailles. (You've installed a lightning rod.) He likes America so much that you forgive him for trying to get commissions on every possible shipment to the rebel army.

NO ONE SAID IT WOULD BE EASY

DESPITE THE SUPPORT OF THESE four men, you face major obstacles to winning a formal French alliance, your ultimate goal. First of all, the French don't want to lose another war or to waste money on a losing struggle. Washington's outmanned, outgunned army has been losing (or, perhaps intelligently, fleeing) more often than winning. The challenge this trend poses, even to your masterful spin skills, keeps growing. When England's General William Howe takes and occupies Philadelphia, you assure the French he'll get bogged down there: "Instead of Howe taking Philadelphia, Philadelphia has taken Howe." (On a personal note, the British captain quartered in your Philly house ends up stealing books, musical instruments, and electrical equipment. You try not to let it get you down.) When Stormont boasts to Vergennes that England has deployed two-thirds of its mighty army and half its navy against America, you bravely insist, "All the better. England will be trapped in the end!" You will eventually be proven right on both counts, but for now France wants more than promises.

Second, the Continental Congress isn't totally behind you: many members distrust France, remembering the last war and feeling no love for French language, religion, and morals. You understand France much better, having visited before and read many French books, and your open-minded outlook makes you more comfortable with the Catholic religion, but you've got to drag the Congress along before you can offer the French a good deal.

Third, you have limited time each day for diplomacy. America needs you to manage *most* of its European business, including passport issuance, financial matters, and military affairs. On the military side, you oversee John Paul Jones, the "father of the US Navy," in his raids on the English; you employ privateers (basically

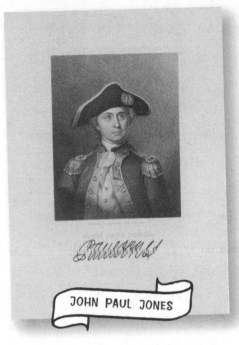

JOHN PAUL JONES

pirates sponsored by America) to keep the enemy navy busy by preying on English merchant ships; and you filter (and mostly reject) the hundreds of European officers who, having been sidelined by peace on their own continent, want positions in the US Army. You've never worked harder, although you do most of your paperwork at night to avoid *seeming* to work hard. Typical image management: in Philadelphia you carted your own paper to show how industrious you

DIDYA KNOW?

John Paul Jones was actually born plain John Paul, the son of a Scottish gardener. He added "Jones" when he became a fugitive from British justice, accused of killing a mutinous sailor. (He swears it was only self-defense.)

were, but *here* you understand that no one respects a grind. The French appreciate excellence only if it appears effortless!

Fourth, your health, at seventy-two, is hardly perfect. The Atlantic crossing covered much of your upper body with pus-filled lumps called boils. The skin disease psoriasis has given you further grief; you took mercury pills for it until they made three of your teeth fall out. Then there's your gout, a painful inflammation in your joints, which will trouble you the rest of your life. Still, you soldier on.

Fifth, you are not alone in your mission. The Congress has actually sent three "commissioners" to France: you, Silas Deane, and Arthur Lee. Deane is generally helpful, but he has just been called home after Lee accused him of cheating on his expenses, and he is showing signs of unhappiness with the new US government. You *hate* Lee, whose deadly combination of lame ideas and nasty temper makes him a menace to your mission: "In sowing suspicions and jealousies, in creating misunderstandings and quarrels among friends, in malice, subtlety, and indefatigable industry, he has I think no equal." Unfortunately, he has two powerful brothers in the Congress, so getting rid of him will not be easy.

A haughty gentleman, born into one of Virginia's richest families, Lee looks down on you as an upstart tradesman. His idiocy is sometimes laughable, as when he tried to order army uniforms in *red* (you know, as in "redcoats"?) because "no troops ever fought so well in any other color." Luckily, your good sense prevailed, and Washington's men dress in blue and brown. But Lee is more dangerous when showing the French how little he trusts them, which only chips away at their crucial goodwill.

Lee tells the Congress that the only way to French hearts (such as they are) is through their pocketbooks. He wants to base America's appeal for help on tobacco and other trade deals, nothing else. But he's wrong: you understand that the French may be greedy, but they're also idealistic. You arrange for the Declaration of Independence and other inspiring documents to be published in French, knowing that many French will embrace America's ideals: "Tyranny is so generally established in the rest of the world that the prospect of an asylum in America for those who love liberty gives general joy, and our cause is esteemed the cause of all mankind." And whenever France does help, you show actual *gratitude*. In return, Vergennes both likes you and trusts you, which allows further progress toward a treaty.

Given how useless Lee is, you're glad to have one skilled worker on your team: Edward Bancroft, whom you've appointed secretary to Deane, Lee, and yourself. Bancroft is a man you respect, a former student of Deane's whom you met in London and used as an information source there from 1773 onward. He's also a doctor and a naturalist, known for documenting the electrical charges generated by the mysterious torpedo fish, which he encountered during an expedition to South America. Your kind of guy!

THE CHOICE

BUT THERE'S A SIXTH DIFFICULTY: spies lurk everywhere—including in your own offices. The French police track everything that happens around you, paying your servants to report all comings and goings. Whatever letters from America make it through the British blockade are intercepted, read, and sometimes destroyed; often you do not hear from the Congress for six months at a stretch.

And those are your *friends'* spies! Your enemies' spies are an even bigger problem. England's local spymaster is Paul Wentworth, an American Loyalist who speaks French fluently, has multiple Paris addresses, and uses more than twenty false names. He seems alarmingly well informed about everything that goes on with you: almost as soon as you've said or written something, England appears to know. Vergennes has scolded you for having such poor security. There must be a mole in your organization, but who? And will he (or she) stop you from getting your treaty with France?

You could investigate Lee; even if he's not the mole,

casting suspicion might get rid of him. You could investigate Bancroft, who's aware of everything that happens in your offices. You could investigate Deane, who seems to be having second thoughts about independence. Or you could investigate no one and wait to see what happens.

WHAT DO YOU DO, BEN? SELECT ONE:

A. Look out for Lee.

Lee *seems* too thick to succeed as a spy. He may be dangerous to America's mission (the French hate him), but probably not on purpose. Your charges of spying would fall flat in any case, because most congressmen see him as a patriot, whereas *you* will never entirely shake their suspicion that you are too friendly with the French (and maybe the English).

You don't like Lee much: "If some of the many enemies he provokes do not kill him sooner, he will die in a madhouse." But what if all that bumbling is just an act, and he's really a master spy?

B. Beware Bancroft.

Unlike Lee, Bancroft is clearly smart. Maybe *too* smart. He's a great worker, quiet and careful, but how much do you really know about him? He spied for *you* in London, so you know he's good at it. Could he be a double agent?

C. Distrust Deane.

Deane is the son of a blacksmith who went on to marry not one but two wealthy widows, both of whom later died. Hmm. What if Lee's right and Deane *has* been fiddling his expenses? Maybe he's got hidden money problems. You know he's been growing increasingly annoyed with the Congress; then again, would a British spy admit that?

D. Interrogate no one.

For a guy whom the CIA will one day call "the Founding Father of Covert Action," you seem pretty laid-back about spycraft. Deane busies himself with codes and invisible inks, but not you. Still, shouldn't you be a *little* more concerned about guarding American secrets?

THE REVEAL

YOU CHOSE . . . **D. Interrogate no one**. You don't bother even *trying* to find the mole. Your policy is "simply this—to be concerned in no affairs that I should blush to have made public, and to do nothing but what spies may see. . . . If I was sure, therefore, that my valet . . . was a spy, as probably he is, I think I should not discharge him for that, if in other respects I liked him."

THE AFTERMATH

DOES THAT APPLY TO YOUR secretary too, Ben? Yes, *Bancroft* is the one betraying you, and with all his customary efficiency. He happens to know spymaster Wentworth from long ago, when he consulted on a plantation that Wentworth owned in South America (small world!). Each Tuesday Bancroft sneaks off to the Tuileries, a park where he leaves dispatches, stuffed in a bottle, dangling inside a hollow tree. He disguises them as letters describing someone's imaginary love life, writing the spy info literally between the lines, in invisible ink. Another Wentworth agent picks them up and leaves a reply, which Bancroft collects later that night. Luckily, his leaks do not help the British much. If anything, he only makes them more anxious about your activities.

Your secretary is so good at this second job (for which he collects a parallel salary and pension from the English!) that his treachery will not be discovered until 1891, when the British Foreign Ministry finally releases his file to research-ers. By then Bancroft will have died rich in England, having made a fortune by importing plant dyes after the war—and by shady stock trading *during* the war. Edward Bancroft: unknown villain of the Revolutionary War.

Deane is innocent, BTW, though he will end up opposing the Revolution. He's been pretty effective so far but is losing faith in the Continental Congress fast and will soon call for abandoning the war. After trying in vain to disprove Lee's charges of embezzlement, he will be exiled from America as a traitor and reduced to poverty. Only in 1841 will Congress decide that Lee's accusations were baseless and pay compensation to Deane's heirs.

One last note on Deane: He will die from a mysterious illness in 1789, just before sailing home from England to clear his name of treason. Historians will speculate that he was poisoned—perhaps by doctor/toxin expert Edward Bancroft, concerned that Deane was planning to unmask *him* as a spy.

Leaking to Win

MAYBE ONE REASON LEAKS BOTHER you so little is that you know how to use them. Having everyone know what you're doing serves your purposes! For example, when news reaches you that America has finally scored a major victory (at Saratoga, using mostly French guns), it gives France evidence that America may end up winning the war after all. (Beaumarchais leaves your office in such a rush to put in his stock trades before anyone *else* hears about Saratoga that he crashes his carriage, breaking his arm.) Within two days, King Louis invites you to resubmit your treaty proposal—info that you know will reach England fast!

England does hear and gets so nervous that Wentworth approaches you to discuss possible peace terms. You welcome him because you know that Vergennes, who's desperate to avoid having Britain and America kiss and make up, will get word of these talks. See, this is how you *use* leaks! As Ambassador Stormont complains to Vergennes, "They play us off against one another. Franklin's natural subtlety gives him a great advantage in such a game." Stormont's right: the risk that you might cut a deal with Wentworth is what finally gets France to stop waffling and commit to a formal treaty. The document, a crucial one in America's history, promises France's continuing help against England and provides formal recognition that America has really taken its place among the independent nations of the world. At last!

You sign the treaty at Versailles in February 1778, wearing not your usual brown coat (which the French find charmingly plain) but rather the same blue velvet suit you wore during your 1774 humiliation in the Cockpit. Why that suit? To "give it a little revenge."

Vergennes is so anxious to make the treaty official that he agrees to announce it (and send Stormont packing) even before the Congress has a chance to approve it (or to mess it up by demanding more concessions).

Congratulations, Ben! You have pulled off one of the greatest diplomatic triumphs ever—without which America could not have won its freedom.

Choice X—1782

LET'S MAKE A
DEAL

THE CHALLENGE

WITH LOTS OF HELP FROM France (thanks to you), America has gradually turned the tide of war against England. But it's not over yet. How can you negotiate the best peace terms without making new enemies for America—or yourself?

THE BACKSTORY

YOU'VE BEEN LIVING LARGE IN that Passy mansion for about five years now. You adore France for its manners and refinement: "This is the civilest nation upon earth." Living here does wonders for your health, too. In 1780, you joked to a friend, "I do not find that I grow any older. Being arrived at seventy, and considering that by traveling further in the same road I should probably be led to the grave, I stopped short, turned about, and walked back again; which having done these four years, you may now call me sixty-six."

John Adams, who's arrived to replace Silas Deane, is scandalized by your lifestyle. He thinks you lazy, not knowing how much you accomplish after midnight. All he sees is that you go out to parties most nights, not getting home until late. Your mornings are filled with visitors, he writes, mostly "women and children, come to have the honor to see the great Franklin, and to have the pleasure of telling stories about his simplicity, his bald head." Your main meal most days is the seven-course, midafternoon "dinner."

Your older grandson (Temple) does useful work in your office, while your younger one (Benny) goes to boarding school in Switzerland. You hang out with lots of scientists and philosophers, but your favorite companions tend to be female—two in particular.

One is Anne Brillon, who lives next door with her husband. A talented musician, she celebrated the Saratoga win by composing a triumphal "March of the Rebels," which will still be played centuries later. She is not yet forty, and there is probably nothing between you but witty flirting, yet you do have a genuinely close relationship. She loves you (as a friend) for "that

gaiety and gallantry that cause all women to love you, because you love them all. . . . You combine the kindest heart with the soundest moral teaching, a lively imagination, and that droll roguishness which shows that the wisest of men allows his wisdom to be broken against the rocks of femininity."

The other woman is Madame Helvétius, widow of a famous philosopher. She lives a bit farther away but is much closer to you in age, about sixty. She's a nonconformist, for sure: she keeps a household of eighteen Angora cats, plus dogs, birds, and several pet philosophers. One American visitor is appalled at the scene there: "She had a little lapdog, who was, next to the doctor"—that's you—"her favorite. This she kissed, and when he wet the floor, she wiped it up with her [dress]." Gross. Still, you've fallen hard for this intelligent and unconventional woman, proposing marriage more than once. Alas, she is too free a spirit to want to tie herself down, even to you.

These two friendships inspire some of your best writing, which you print on your own little press at Passy (originally installed in your office to produce passports and loan documents). You base an amusing "Dialogue between the Gout and Mr. Franklin" on a poem by Madame Brillon in which the disease says you should be *grateful* to it—because it recedes when you eat less and exercise more, leading you to a healthier lifestyle. In "The Elysian Fields," you write Madame Helvétius that you dreamed of visiting the afterlife, where it turns out her late husband has married Deborah. "Let us revenge ourselves," you propose, and get married, too! You use these and other pieces to entertain your friends and also to practice French, writing them in both languages side by side.

But life since signing the French treaty has not all been fun and games. You've continued to oversee the American war effort in Europe, so you share in the glory when John Paul Jones, commanding America's *Bonhomme Richard* (donated by your host, Chaumont, and named after Poor Richard, in your honor), defeats a better-armed British ship. The English captain thinks Jones is beaten and demands that he surrender, but Jones famously declares, "I have not yet begun to fight!" He then boards the enemy ship and captures it just as his own is in danger of sinking. Well done!

HATERS GONNA HATE

ON A LESS PLEASANT NOTE, you continue to have problems with office politics. You beat out Lee to win from the Congress the new position of minister plenipotentiary (basically ambassador) to France, but Lee stuck around, continuing to backstab you and to criticize you as old, lazy, unreliable, and soft on the French. You choose to ignore him and his friends: "They quarrel *at* me rather than *with* me, for I will not quarrel with

them. . . . This I think most prudent for a public character, but I suspect myself of being a little malicious in it, for I imagine they are more vexed by such neglect than they would be by a tart reply."

Meanwhile, John Adams is jealous of your celebrity, whining that you "have a monopoly of reputation here and an indecency in displaying it." He does not like you one bit, saying he feels for you "no other sentiments than contempt and abhorrence." Then again, this is the same prickly guy who once called George Washington a mutton head. But he's smarter than Lee, which actually makes him more of a threat to you.

Adams has little fondness for the French, either. He finds their morals lax and even calls your valuable friend Lafayette a "mongrel character" whose "unlimited ambition" has him "panting for glory." He annoys your allies with blunt demands; it doesn't help that his French is no better than yours, for all his earnest efforts to improve it. (Unlike you, he pores over grammar books and vocab lists.) Vergennes, thoroughly turned off by Adams's pushiness, has disinvited him from court with a curt note that "the King has not stood in need of your promptings to tend to the needs of the United States." What a contrast from your smooth effectiveness!

Last year, Lee and his allies succeeded in getting the Congress to vote on having you recalled. You won the vote easily, but you'd had enough infighting and still submitted your resignation. "I have passed my seventy-fifth year," you wrote. "I do not know that my mental faculties are impaired; perhaps I shall be the last to discover that." Your long decades of public service had given you "honor sufficient to satisfy any reasonable ambition, and I have no other left but that of repose, which I hope Congress will grant me."

But, as you probably hoped, the Congress wouldn't accept your resignation. They were horrified by the thought of your leaving France and practically begged you to stay. So there! "I call this continuance an honor," you write a friend, "and I really esteem it to be greater than my first appointment, when I consider that all the interest of my enemies [was] not sufficient to prevent it."

Vergennes pushed hard for you, sending a message to the Congress that your performance has been "as zealous and patriotic as it is wise and circumspect." With his help, you've even gained an additional position! Now that Britain's general has surrendered at Yorktown (a victory largely made possible by French troops and the French navy), the war has clearly turned in America's favor, so the Congress has given you (along with Adams and the clever New Yorker John Jay) the job of negotiating peace with England.

FUN FACT

This mission is a sort of homecoming for Jay. His grandfather, a French Protestant, came to America fleeing religious persecution from an earlier King Louis. Awkward!

THE CHOICE

NOW THINGS START TO GET *really* complicated. First, two rival British ministers have sent negotiators, so you naturally pick the one you like better. Luckily, he's the one working for your old friend Lord Shelburne (on whose estate, more than a decade ago, you did your magic trick of smoothing the waters with oil). Even luckier, Shelburne soon wins the power struggle in London, becoming prime minister, second in power only to the king.

Second, the English can't officially negotiate a treaty with rebels, and you refuse to bargain until they've recognized American independence. Eventually, they agree to negotiate officially, basically yielding that point, but other issues could be tougher. How to handle the property of American Loyalists, for example, anti-independence families who are now refugees in England or Canada? And how about compensation for American civilians injured by Britain's Indian allies? America wants a free trade agreement, fishing rights off the Canadian coast, and more. How much will the British concede?

Third, you've long assured Vergennes (and the Congress has instructed) that you will make no deal with England unless France approves it. On the other hand, France has its own agenda, and you might get better terms from the British if you make a "separate peace" with them.

Fourth, your fellow commissioners, Adams and Jay, have their own ideas. They are more flexible than you with regard to England, but both distrust the French. Jay bears a century-old grudge against them thanks to his grandfather the refugee. And Adams, after his big brush-off from Vergennes, is so rabid that you tell the Congress you hope "the ravings of a certain mischievous madman against France and its ministers, which I hear every day, will not be regarded in America." It's hard enough negotiating with England; you've got two adversaries closer and just as tough.

So, do you honor your promise to France and refuse a separate peace with England? Do you hang tough on terms with England? How about with Adams and Jay?

WHAT DO YOU DO, BEN? SELECT ONE:

A. Keep your promise to France.

You love the French, and they've spent huge sums helping your fledgling country. You're also a man who likes to keep his promises. If you break yours to Vergennes, will the French ever forgive you?

B. Tough it out with England.

Whatever treaty you sign, with or without France, will be complicated. So many details to negotiate! The English have basically lost the war; how can you now make sure they don't win the peace? You blame them for their tyranny, the bloodshed they've caused, their insults to you, and maybe even your estrangement from William. Now that you have them where you want them, how lightly are you prepared to let them off?

C. Butt heads with Adams and Jay.

Adams pretty clearly can't stand you, and he seems to have gotten Jay to agree with him on many issues. Technically they outnumber you, but you're Ben Franklin! Will you let them push you around when America's vital interests hang in the balance?

D. Sign a separate peace with England.

Promises are important, but America's future is at stake here. Vergennes must ultimately do what's best for France, and you likewise have your own responsibility to America. You don't have to be anti-French to understand that France and Spain have their eyes on land west of the United States, both to gain territory and to (in your words) "coop us up." If you give your allies a veto over any deal with

England, they might end up extracting for themselves some barrier territory between the states and the Mississippi River. Knowing better than most people the value of that land for America's future, will you agree with Adams and Jay that you should sign a separate peace with England?

THE REVEAL

YOU CHOSE . . . **D. Sign a separate peace with England**. This agreement, so masterfully negotiated, will go down in history as the Treaty of Paris. The war that you helped win is now over. America, thanks in part to you, has officially won its freedom!

SIGNING OF THE TREATY OF PARIS

John Jay and John Adams appear on the left here, your grandson Temple on the right. The painting is unfinished because the British signers refused to pose!

THE AFTERMATH

IN YOUR DESIRE TO END the war, you show flexibility toward all parties. (Luckily, on most issues you're not that far apart from Adams and Jay.) Even Adams is surprised by how easy you are to work with: "[He] has gone on with us in entire unanimity and harmony and has been able and useful, both by his sagacity and his reputation, in the whole negotiation."

Against the English, you do get your way on some points (like drawing America's western boundary at the Mississippi, not farther east), and Adams succeeds in demanding that private debts to British merchants should not be renounced as part of the treaty. (He may be a hothead, but he does have to keep in mind the merchants of Boston, who don't want to risk retaliation by their British customers.)

You even stick to your guns on one issue where Adams and Jay were willing to favor England: you insist there will be no paying American Loyalists for property the rebels confiscated or destroyed. Why do you take such a hard line here? One reason is to show the Congress that you are not being soft on English sympathizers. But another may be more personal: you are still steamed at William, whose loyalty to England stung you as a personal betrayal. (His work as royal governor and his defiance of the Congress still make some at home suspect *your* patriotism, so you also want to leave no doubt about where your allegiance really lies.)

You generally bend when possible, though, because you want this war to end. You hate the war's hatred, the needless cost, and especially the bloodshed. As you write to Polly Stevenson, "All wars are follies, very expensive and very mischievous ones. When will mankind be convinced of this, and agree to settle their differences by arbitration? Were they to do it, even by the cast of a die, it would be better than by fighting and destroying each other."

One demand you must give up: getting compensation for Americans victimized by the redcoats and their Indian allies. It's painful, because you've really tried on this point. You even printed at Passy a phony issue of a Boston newspaper, featuring shocking "fake news" of scalps, *bales* of American scalps, shipped by the Seneca tribe to King George. To make the fake issue more convincing, you included made-up ads—a missing horse announced here, a house for sale there. "The *form* may perhaps not be genuine," you admitted to a friend, "but the *substance* is truth."

Pardon, Vergennes!

YOU KNOW YOU'RE DOUBLE-CROSSING VER-GENNES, so you write him a very pretty apology—once the treaty with England is signed. Your mistake, you explain, was due to your inexperience at diplomacy (yeah, right), and you hope he won't let this little misunderstanding drive a wedge between your two countries, since King Louis clearly cares so much about America's future. America and France still need each other, you tell him; why give England the satisfaction of seeing you split up? That's called putting the best face on a bad situation.

Vergennes still goes ballistic, writing back that your "abrupt" signing with England is not "agreeable to the King." Your apology does not stop him from sending an informal protest to the Congress, which considers reprimanding you for ignoring its instruction to give France a veto. In the end, though, no one can argue with your success: you have managed to extract much better terms through your separate peace. France even keeps providing loans, if only to avoid America's becoming closer to England or defaulting on the huge sums you've already borrowed.

Vergennes, angry both personally and for France's sake, predicts that "we shall be but poorly paid for all that we have done for the United States," and in the short term he is right. Not only has France spent enormous sums on this war, taxing its own citizens, but now America is shining forth as an example of liberty—to which the French people are not blind. In 1789, they will rise in rebellion themselves, and King Louis (together with many of your French friends) will lose his life in the bloody, chaotic French Revolution.

But in the longer term, Vergennes is wrong. America will come to France's aid in two world wars, thus repaying the debt you felt so keenly. In 1917, an American officer, part of a huge force sent to rescue France, will utter words you'd appreciate: "Lafayette, we are here."

DIDYA KNOW?

Lafayette himself lived to 1834. In 1824, he received a huge hero's welcome when he visited America, touring all twenty-four states as the country's guest.

Ben Franklin, Master of the Game

ERTAIN HISTORIANS WILL SAY YOU gamed this delicate treaty situation like a chess master, because your strategy was so excellent *and* chess plays such a major role in your life. How major? Major major:

★ You picked up the game early on and since then play whenever you get the chance.

★ In your twenties, you and a friend even learned Italian by making the loser of each chess game study a new piece of grammar or vocabulary. "As we played pretty equally we thus beat each other into that language."

★ In your fifties and sixties, you played game after game in the coffeehouses of London.

★ In 1774, your secret London peace talks, with that same Richard Howe who later commanded England's navy against America, happened under cover of chess dates with his sister.

★ In Paris, you often dally at the chessboard past midnight, once putting off an urgent dispatch from the Congress until you've finished your game.

★ Another time, playing against a pretty French duchess, you capture her king without the usual courtesy of first announcing it's in check. "Ah, we do not take kings so," she protests. "We do in America," comes your famous reply.

★ You play a public match in Paris against the Mechanical Turk, the incredible moving statue that almost never loses— not even to you. (Later, the "machine" turns out to contain a really, really small and skilled human player.)

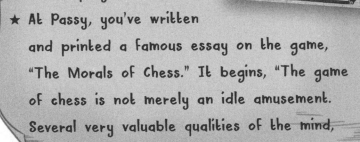

I've got a secret weapon!

★ At Passy, you've written and printed a famous essay on the game, "The Morals of Chess." It begins, "The game of chess is not merely an idle amusement. Several very valuable qualities of the mind, useful in the course of human life, are to be acquired or strengthened by it, so as to become habits, ready on all occasions. For life is a kind of chess, in which we have often points to gain, and competitors or adversaries to contend with." You argue that chess can teach players to plan ahead, not to move too quickly, to consider all options before making a choice—and to resist getting too discouraged (or overconfident), because situations that look one way often turn out another.

Given the game's importance to your outlook on life, it's only natural that some historians will say you showed your great chess skill during these treaty talks. They're mistaken, though: given all the bluffing, the unknowns, the multiple players at the table, and the importance of luck, this treaty game's really a whole lot more like poker. You, Ben, are a man of many skills.

LIBERTY
FOR ALL?

THE CHALLENGE

WITH MASTERFUL NEGOTIATING, YOU'VE helped America win independence from its British overlords. Now every American is free—except the enslaved ones. Wait, what?

THE BACKSTORY

AFTER NEGOTIATING A SUCCESSFUL END to the war, you stuck around, enjoying the pleasures of

Paris for another couple of years. So many people asked you for advice about moving to America that you published a pamphlet telling them they must be prepared to work hard. Nobles, especially, you warned not to expect special treatment in a country where "people do not enquire of a stranger, What is he?, but, What can he do?" Long live America!

On the science front, you invented bifocal glasses, fitting half lenses from two pairs into one frame so the wearer could see far or near without changing spectacles. You were also thrilled to witness the first manned flights of hot-air balloons. When an

FUN FACT

The first manned balloon took off in November 1783. Its creators, the Montgolfier brothers, were the Wright brothers of their day. Are you surprised that their partner in designing this balloon was a leading maker of wallpaper?

unimaginative spectator asked what use they could be, your classic answer became famous: "What is the use of a newborn baby?" You may be a practical man, but you've got more imagination than most.

Thomas Jefferson arrived to take over your responsibilities in France. Frenchmen, meeting him, would ask if he was the one replacing you. Jefferson's standard response was "No one can replace him, sir; I am only his successor."

On your way to America, you spent four days in England, mostly seeing old friends. Your least pleasant meeting? With your son William, living there in bitter exile. William tried to mend fences with you, even selling his New Jersey farm to his son Temple for almost nothing at your request. Sadly, you parted on frosty terms and will never see each other again in this life.

Uniting the United States

YOU RETURNED TO AMERICA a hero, settling in with Sally and her family at your house. The country was thrilled to be free but was already running into serious problems, many arising from the Articles of Confederation, which kept the federal government weak. The federal government couldn't levy taxes, for example, so it had little money with which to pay expenses—including the army.

It was bad enough for the United States to be broke, but even worse that they were not fully united. Under the Articles, America was a nation in some respects but in other ways was more like a loose alliance of states (each with its own currency!). The country got a wake-up call in 1786 from Shays's Rebellion, a fierce uprising of Massachusetts war veterans and farmers. Although the re-

volt eventually failed, the government's slow and feeble response exposed the nation's weakness.

DIDYA KNOW?

Daniel Shays (left) was a farmhand who fought at Lexington and Concord, Bunker Hill, and Saratoga. After he was wounded and left the army, his creditors dragged him into court because the government still hadn't coughed up his back pay. Doesn't seem fair, does it?

Now, to fix the rickety framework set by the Articles, you and fifty-four other men have gathered in the Philadelphia statehouse for the Constitutional Convention. Bad news: it's summer, as it was when you signed the Declaration of Independence in that same fateful room, and once again the place is sweltering.

A Good Constitution for Your Age

YOU ARE BY FAR THE oldest delegate. In your eighty-one years, you've visited many countries and learned much about politics and human nature. You've been pondering forms of government since before that conference in Albany, thirty-three years ago. Delegates often seek your counsel under the mulberry tree in your backyard, just a few blocks from where the convention is meeting. You also hold the highest position in Pennsylvania, president of the executive council. But, despite your vast experience, you're one of the quietest delegates, often writing down your opinions for others to read on your behalf.

The ideas you do suggest are not winning many fans at the convention. You propose an executive council

THE STATE-HOUSE IN PHILADELPHIA 1776

instead of a president, for example, with its members unpaid in order to avoid the corruption you witnessed in England: "In all cases of public service, the less the profit, the greater the honor." Sorry, no dice.

Your most important contribution is helping to bring about a compromise on the convention's most hotly debated topic: representation. The large states push to apportion legislators among the states based on population (naturally), while the small states (also naturally) prefer equal representation for all states.

First, you make a long appeal urging the delegates to

be flexible in their views. "Declarations of a fixed opinion," you say, "and of determined resolution never to change, neither enlighten nor convince us." Having laid the groundwork for compromise, you then offer potential solutions, none of which catch on—for instance, that large states give up some land to smaller ones to make them all around the same size.

On the same day, though, Connecticut's Roger Sherman presents a more practical proposal. What if there were *two* houses in the legislature, with the House of Representatives apportioned by population and the Senate representing all states equally? At first it's voted down, but you decide to promote the "Connecticut Compromise," explaining it in clear terms and playing up its benefits for every state. The delegates approve the plan, in great part because of your influence and reputation. Good work, Ben!

THE CHOICE

THE CONSTITUTIONAL CONVENTION IS GOING well, thanks in part to you, but it has been dancing around one particular issue that bothers you. That issue: slavery. About one in six Americans is enslaved—more than one in three within the Southern states. The Declaration of Independence called it "self-evident" (your word, remember?) that "all men are created equal," but "life, liberty, and the pursuit of happiness" are still reserved for only *some* Americans.

Even you, Ben, have been part of the slave system. You've owned slaves, who helped in your household and in your printing shop. In your newspaper, you printed ads for both the sale and capture of slaves, even though you also printed Quaker antislavery essays. You came out against American slavery in your 1751 "Observations," but not because of its terrible injustice. Instead, you believed the colonies didn't need to import any additional labor, and you thought slavery bad for *whites:* in slaveholding families, "children become proud, disgusted with labor, and being educated in idleness, are rendered unfit to get a living by industry."

To be SOLD,

TWO likely healthy Negroe Women, one 20, the other 15 Years of Age, and have both had the Small-pox and Measles, well acquainted with House-work, and are very fit for Town or Country Business. For further Particulars, enquire of John Hall, at the Wheat Sheaf, or of Richard Morris, near the Court-House, Philadelphia. ¶ 5s. Tbc.

N. B. A Woman with a good Breast of Milk, can be well recommended, wants a Wet Nurse's Place. Enquire of said Morris.

In those days you unfortunately still shared many of the prejudices of your time, even writing that "every slave is by nature a thief." In the early 1760s, though, you learned to take a more enlightened view. You visited (and donated to) schools for black children. You saw enough there to develop a "higher opinion of the natural capacities of the black race," calling their learning ability "in every respect equal to that of white children."

In the 1770s, you began to have even more serious doubts about slavery's morality. You wrote an unsigned piece for the *London Chronicle* in which you criticized England for helping to introduce slavery to the colonies. Although the British felt proud of having banned slavery within England, you called them hypocritical for profiting from the slave trade ("this pestilential detestable traffic in the bodies and souls of men") and from slavery in the colonies (featuring "excessive labor, bad nourishment, uncomfortable accommodation, and broken spirits"). You argued passionately that the great British pleasure of drinking sweetened tea was not worth the pain and dehumanization endured by "our fellow creatures" who produced the sugar.

So here you are at the Constitutional Convention, drafting the document intended to shape American government and society. You're now president of the Pennsylvania Abolition Society! So do you go public at the convention, trying to end slavery through the Constitution? If you wait until after the convention, do you push for immediate abolition, eventual abolition, or just the prohibition of slavery in any *new* American territories? Whatever you do, this issue is *not* going away.

A. Fight to end slavery via the Constitution.

The Constitution is the blueprint for America's future. How can you permit the monstrous inhumanity of slavery to remain a feature within that blueprint?

B. After the convention, press for immediate abolition.

The Southern delegates are sworn to prevent the adoption of any constitution that ends or even limits slavery. Without a new constitution, the federal government will not be strong enough to survive for long, let alone enforce a ban on slavery. Maybe you should wait until the Constitution is in place and *then* push for immediate emancipation of the enslaved?

C. Argue for eventual abolition.

You know slavery is wrong, but one of the terrible things about it is that it deprives many enslaved people of the knowledge and experience that they would need to thrive in free society. Perhaps some intermediate steps, some paving of the way, could both make the slaveholders more willing to yield peacefully and, at the same time, help to prepare the slaves for life as full citizens.

D. Oppose only the spread of slavery.

The slave states are adamant about holding on to their evil institution. If you don't want to risk all-out war among the states, could it make sense simply to press for a law against slavery in any states where it does not already exist?

THE REVEAL

YOU CHOSE . . . **C. Argue for eventual abolition.** You wait until after the convention, then push for eventual abolition. Originally, you *want* to propose the inclusion in the Constitution of a moral statement against slavery, clarifying that the country would eventually free its slaves. But other delegates convince you that Southern fury at such a motion could throw the convention into an uproar, endanger the Constitution, and perhaps threaten the unity of the country itself.

Reluctantly, you decide that silence is a price you are willing to pay (for now) if it buys Southern support for a strong central government.

THE AFTERMATH

IRONICALLY, SLAVERY *DOES* BECOME a hot topic at the convention, but not because of abolition. Here's the question: If every state will be represented partly according to population, should slaves be counted as property or as people? Because everyone wants a greater say in the House of Representatives, Southerners (ironically) argue that of course slaves are people, whereas Northerners (even those who oppose slavery!) want slaves treated as property. The two sides finally hammer out the infamous Three-Fifths Compromise, which essentially counts a slave as three-fifths of a human being. The compromise is absurd and cruel, but most delegates think it's the only way to get the document approved.

You put your full weight behind the Constitution once it's drafted, knowing it can always be amended when Americans are ready to abolish slavery. For now, you give a long speech on the convention's last day, explaining that you support "this Constitution because I expect no better, and because I am not sure, that it is not the best." Although you don't "entirely approve of this Constitution," you urge the delegates to set aside their objections and vote in favor, for the sake of unanimity; and every state's delegation votes yes. Partly because of your prestige and sponsorship, Ben, the Constitution will go on to be ratified by every state and will give America a firm foundation for centuries to come. As for slavery, the nation will have to face that issue later.

Fighting the Good Fight

OON AFTER THE CONVENTION FINISHES, you write a declaration for your Pennsylvania Abolition Society that "slavery is such an atrocious debasement of human nature" that ending it without due care "may sometimes open a source of serious evils." You believe in moderation, after all, and you recognize that abolition, *because* it is such a major change, must be undertaken gradually. Not only does the country need to get used to the idea step by step, but plans must be formed to give the freed slaves a fair start in their new lives. Because a slave who "has long been treated as a brute animal" has to overcome handicaps as a free citizen, your society will work not only to free slaves over time but also to help them fit into society once freed.

In 1790, now eighty-four, you act more forcefully against slavery than ever before. You're not getting any younger, and you don't care if you need to burn some bridges in this just cause. You write a radical petition pushing the newly elected Congress for an end to slavery throughout the country. The petition argues that Congress was made for the purpose of giving "the blessings of Liberty to the people of the United States," so these blessings should be awarded "without distinction of color to all descriptions of people."

Because you are ahead of your time, your petition faces harsh criticism from congressmen and voters alike. Southern politicians argue vehemently against your progressive ideas, using the Bible and supposed natural law as justification. They see you and your abolitionist friends as dangers to the Southern way of life, to conventional order and stability. Unfortunately for the enslaved and for America, this problem is only going to get harder to solve.

One Last Prank with a Point

KNOWING THAT, YOU USE EVERY ounce of your remaining strength to bring the day of abolition closer. In typical Franklin fashion, you respond to your critics with scathing satire. March 1790: you write a letter to the *Federal Gazette* under the name Historicus. You are frail and very ill now; this is the last public letter you'll ever write, so devoting it to slavery shows how important the issue is to you.

The letter reprints a supposed speech given by the (fictional) Algerian official Sidi Mehemet Ibrahim in the late 1600s, when Algeria and other North African countries routinely traded in white Christian slaves. Ibrahim is defending Algerian slavery with arguments amazingly similar to those used by Southern congressmen to defend *American* slavery.

Southern politicians often argue that (1) only people originating from a hot place like Africa can work hard in the Southern climate, (2) white people are doing slaves a favor by exposing them to Christianity and "civilized" customs, (3) revered biblical figures like Abraham owned slaves, so the institution is permitted by the Bible, and (4) elimination of the slave system would cause an economic collapse.

You parody these claims brilliantly, showing just how ridiculous proslavery arguments are by mirroring them through a Muslim lens. Ibrahim justifies slavery with the Quran instead of the Bible and points out that Christians should feel lucky to be "brought into a land where the Sun of Islamism gives forth its Light, and shines in full Splendor" and to be getting "acquainted with the true Doctrine, and thereby saving their immortal Souls." The South's other arguments are likewise mimicked, and Historicus dryly reports that the Algerians decided to keep slavery around. Which, despite your best efforts, is what the Americans decide as well—for now.

But for the next seven decades, limiting the *expansion* of slavery will be the best abolitionists can achieve. The first limits are set in 1787 itself, when the Continental Congress passes the Northwest Ordinance, under which the Northwest Territory (east of the Mississippi River, south of the Great Lakes, and northwest of the Ohio River) will forever escape the stain of slavery. And the South *agrees* to that provision only to prevent the new territory from growing tobacco, which Southern planters see as their crop (and as too labor-intensive to grow without slaves).

Time and again over the coming years, North and South will quarrel over whether new states should allow slavery. The South will threaten to secede each time, thus winning a series of compromises that spread slavery to *some* regions—enough to keep the balance of power between slave and free states more or less even. In 1861, though, that cycle will finally break, and a bloody, cataclysmic war will settle the slavery issue once and for all.

Congress should have listened to you, Ben.

"LET ALL MEN KNOW
THEE . . ."

SOON AFTER YOU PUBLISHED YOUR parting shot on slavery, the masterful Sidi Mehemet Ibrahim letter, your health took a quick turn for the worse. You died on April 17, 1790, surrounded by your daughter Sally, her husband, your grandsons Temple and Benny, and Polly Stevenson, your London landlady's daughter, who was like a second daughter to you.

Twenty thousand mourners, the largest gathering at any American funeral to date, came to pay their respects. Clergymen of every faith in Philadelphia led the procession, showing how universally loved you were. The French declared three days of national mourning, an honor never given to any other foreigner, and an official there called you a "mighty genius" who was "able to conquer both thunderbolts and tyrants."

The House of Representatives voted that its members would wear mourning badges for a monthlong tribute. The Senate decided not to follow suit, under the influence of men who remembered you with spite rather than respect: John Adams, Arthur Lee's brother, and Southern senators who resented your attacks on slavery. The nation, though, remembers you as the hero you were.

As a young printer in 1728, you drafted your own epitaph:

The Body of
B. Franklin, Printer,
(Like the cover of an old book,
Its contents worn out,
And stripped of its lettering and gilding)
Lies here, food for worms.
But the work shall not be lost:
For it will (as he believed) appear once more,
In a new and more elegant edition,
Revised and corrected
By the Author.

By "the Author," of course, you meant your Creator, but in another sense you became your *own* author. Not only did you create a world-famous public image, but you literally wrote your own history through your globally bestselling autobiography, which was published after your death. Your upbeat account of your own life artfully left out or glossed over much of the negative and instead emphasized the positive, at least as you saw it.

As an older man, you went with a simpler and more modest epitaph: "Benjamin and Deborah Franklin." With your gravestone, you finally reunited yourself, in name and place, with your steadfast wife. In the end, despite how little time you spent with Deborah in later life, you did recognize the importance of your marriage.

The truth is, despite having been the jolliest Founding Father and the best at "networking," you kept a certain emotional distance from friends and even most family members. It seems you followed Poor Richard's advice to "Let all men know thee, but no man know thee thoroughly." As well liked as you were, as carefully as you explained yourself to anyone who'd listen, you still managed to remain a man of mystery.

Here's another contradiction: while you embodied America's can-do spirit, lived its rags-to-riches dream, and played a major role in unifying the United States, you were also the most European of all the Founding Fathers. You spent more than twenty important years in London and Paris, happily immersing yourself in their cosmopolitan cultures and social hierarchies. And so you, who to Europe represented the American frontier spirit, raised a son who identified more with England and a grandson who was most comfortable in France. (Temple lived, died, and was buried there.)

The decisions you made reflect yet *more* paradoxes: you devoted great effort to being a pleasant companion and getting along with people, yet you made a striking number of fierce enemies. You published bestselling books of wisdom, yet you never fully understood the passions of people who lacked your calm sense of reason. You spent most of your life wealthy, yet to the end you championed the middle class: your will left large sums to the cities of Boston and Philadelphia, sums that for two hundred years funded loans to help countless young artisans and tradespeople start their careers. Later writers accused you of being obsessed with wealth, but you chose to stop working midway through your life because you had enough money for your (relatively selfless) purposes.

Despite your enjoyment of European capitals, Ben, you were an American through and through. Late in life, you sent a half-joking but extremely revealing letter to Sally, claiming that the bald eagle was the wrong bird to symbolize America. You called it "a bird of bad moral character," known for violence and stealing food from other animals. Instead, you wrote, why not the turkey? "For in truth the turkey is in comparison a much more respectable bird, and . . . a true original native of America. He is besides, tho' a little vain and silly, a bird of courage, and would not hesitate to attack a Grenadier of the British Guards who should presume to invade his farm yard with a red coat on."

Does that say more about America, Ben, or about you? *You* were not a fighter by nature, but your true bravery came out when you saw the strong mistreating the weak. Perhaps because you'd experienced such wrongs yourself (from your brother James, the British, and other authority figures), you saved your greatest passion for protecting the less powerful from their oppressors: peaceful Indians from the Paxton Boys, innocent colonists from English overlords, enslaved Africans from cruel owners. America, too, believes in defending the weak against the strong.

You might occasionally have been a little vain, and your later critics said you lacked depth, just as some commentators call American culture shallow and materialistic. It's true that your writing never dug deep into the human condition or scientific theory. But that was because your greatest ambition was to be *useful* in the here and now. America, too, aspires to be a force for good in the world.

The turkey *is* a "respectable bird," Ben, and you were a most respectable man. You deserve respect for your genius, for your humor and generosity of spirit, for your belief in justice and social mobility, and for your stunning contributions to America and all humanity. The world, Ben Franklin, needs more like you.

BEN'S FAMILY

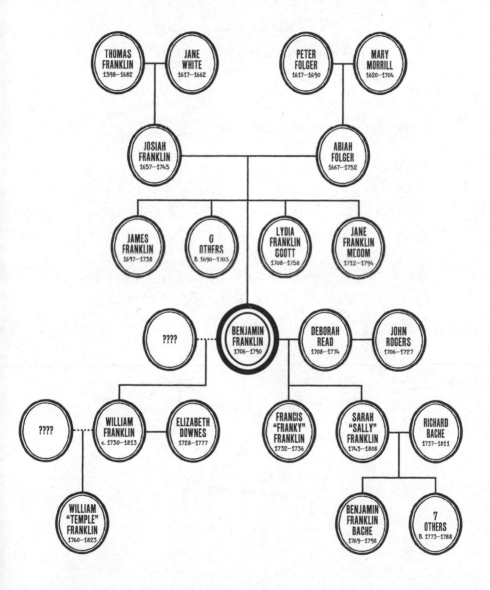

A TIMELINE OF BEN'S LIFE

SPOILER ALERT: Don't read this timeline until you've walked with Ben through the eleven major "crossroads" in this book. Otherwise, you won't get the fun of figuring out his choices for yourself!

1706: Born in Boston, Massachusetts, on January 17 to Josiah Franklin and Abiah Folger

1718: Began apprenticing for his brother James, a local printer

1722: Penned first "Silence Dogood" letter, which appeared in the *New-England Courant,* the paper his brother published

1723: Ran away from his apprenticeship in Boston and headed to Philadelphia

1724: Traveled to London and found work in printing

1726: Created a self-improvement plan based on thirteen virtues of moral perfection; left London and returned to Philadelphia

1727: Formed the Junto, a group of tradesmen who

discussed commercial, political, and philosophical matters

1730: Became sole publisher of the *Pennsylvania Gazette*

1730: Entered into a common-law marriage with Deborah Read; son William born, mother unknown

1732: Son Francis born; penned first volume of *Poor Richard's Almanack*

1736: Son Francis died of smallpox

1743: Daughter Sarah ("Sally") born; created the American Philosophical Society

1747: Organized a Pennsylvania militia

1748: Retired from printing and began spending his time on scientific experiments, writing, and civic projects

1751: Wrote "Observations Concerning the Increase of Mankind, Peopling of Countries, Etc."; elected to the Pennsylvania Assembly; cofounded Pennsylvania Hospital, the first hospital in the colonies

1752: Kite experiment proved that electricity exists in storm clouds

1753: Became deputy postmaster general for the colonies; awarded the Copley Medal of the Royal Society of London for his research in electricity

1754: Drafted the Albany Plan, hoping to unify the

colonies; *Gazette* published the "Join, or Die" cartoon, the first recorded political cartoon in American history

1757: Became the Pennsylvania Assembly's agent to the British government and traveled to London

1758: Published *The Way to Wealth*

1762: Returned to Philadelphia from London

1764: Lost assembly seat; returned to London

1766: Helped repeal the Stamp Act

1774: Wife, Deborah, died

1775: Returned to America from London; became one of the first members of the Second Continental Congress and its Committee of Secret Correspondence, the first foreign intelligence operation in the colonies

1776: Assisted in drafting the Declaration of Independence; helped Thomas Paine publish "Common Sense"; appointed one of three commissioners to France

1778: Negotiated Treaty of Alliance with France; appointed Minister to France

1783: Treaty of Paris signed by Ben, John Adams, and John Jay, establishing peace with England on favorable terms

1787: Signed the Constitution; became president of the Pennsylvania Abolition Society

1790: Signed petition pushing the newly elected Congress for an end to slavery throughout the country; died

WHO'S WHO

John Adams—lawyer from Massachusetts; Ben's fellow diplomat in France; second president of the United States (1797–1801)

Benjamin Franklin Bache—son of Sally Franklin and Richard Bache; grandson of Ben

Richard Bache—shopkeeper; husband of Sally Franklin

Edward Bancroft—doctor and naturalist; secretary to Ben, Silas Deane, and Arthur Lee during their commission to France

Pierre de Beaumarchais—French playwright, watchmaker, musician, and financier; helped convince King Louis XVI to assist America financially at the start of the Revolutionary War

Andrew Bradford—Philadelphia printer and newspaper publisher

Anne Brillon—French musician and close friend of Ben's during his time in France

Jacques de Chaumont—French noble and businessman who hosted Ben at his mansion in the Paris suburbs

Silas Deane—Ben's fellow commissioner to France, along with Arthur Lee

John Dickinson—wealthy Pennsylvania politician; Ben's rival in Pennsylvania Assembly

Elizabeth Downes—wife of William Franklin

Abiah Folger—Ben's mother

Francis Franklin—son of Ben and Deborah Read; died from smallpox at the age of four

James Franklin—printer; one of Ben's older brothers, to whom he was apprenticed

Jane Franklin—Ben's younger sister and favorite sibling

Josiah Franklin—Ben's father; Puritan maker of soap and candles

Sarah "Sally" Franklin—daughter of Ben and Deborah Read

William Franklin—son of Ben (identity of mother unknown, but was raised by Deborah); royal governor of New Jersey from 1762; became estranged from Ben at start of the Revolutionary War

William Temple Franklin—Ben's grandson; illegitimate son of William Franklin; identity of mother unknown

George III—King of Great Britain beginning in 1760

John Hancock—president of the Continental Congress and a signer of the Declaration of Independence

Madame Helvétius—close friend of Ben's during his time in France; Ben proposed marriage more than once, but she declined

Richard Howe—commander of British naval forces during the Revolution

Thomas Hutchinson—friend who helped Ben garner support for the Albany Plan; royal governor of Massachusetts

John Jay—alongside John Adams and Ben, negotiated peace with England after the Revolutionary War

Thomas Jefferson—principal drafter of the Declaration of Independence; Ben's successor as minister to France; third president of the United States (1801–09)

John Paul Jones—born in Scotland; known as the Father of the US Navy

Samuel Keimer—Philadelphia printer; Ben's employer and later rival

Sir William Keith—governor of Pennsylvania colony; gave Ben his first ticket to London

Marquis de Lafayette (Marie-Joseph Paul Yves Roch Gilbert du Motier)—wealthy French aristocrat who fought for American independence

Arthur Lee—Ben's fellow commissioner to France, along with Silas Deane

Louis XVI—King of France beginning in 1774

Thomas Paine—author of "Common Sense," which Ben helped to publish

John Penn—governor of Pennsylvania; nephew of Thomas Penn

Thomas Penn—head of the wealthy Penn family after the death of his father, William Penn; Ben's enemy as proprietor of Pennsylvania

Joseph Priestley—British scientist; close friend to Ben

Deborah Read—common-law wife of Ben and mother of Francis and Sally

Margaret Stevenson—London widow who rented rooms to Ben

Polly Stevenson—daughter of Margaret Stevenson

Lord Stormont—Britain's ambassador to France

Comte de Vergennes—French foreign minister; Ben's main contact at Versailles

Paul Wentworth—spy for England; American loyalist

BEN: INNOVATOR AND ORGANIZER

Ben, you were a true trailblazer in doing good for society. Here is a (short) list of your historic firsts.

- You established the **Library Company of Philadelphia** with help from your fellow Junto members in 1731. This became the first subscription library in the colonies, where subscribers could pay a base fee and then a smaller, annual fee to maintain the library. Eventually, nonmembers were allowed to borrow books. The Library Company of Philadelphia remained the largest public library in the United States until the end of the 1800s.
- You formed the **Union Fire Company of Philadelphia** in 1736, which was the first volunteer firefighting organization in the history of the city.
- To "improve the common stock of knowledge" as you so desired, you formed the **American Philosophical Society** in 1743.

- Though you didn't attend college yourself, you were an advocate of higher learning. In 1749, you helped to establish America's fifth college, the **Academy of Philadelphia**, later known as the University of Pennsylvania. You were president of the Academy from 1749 to 1755.

- In 1751, you cofounded **Pennsylvania Hospital**, the first hospital in the colonies, which opened in 1752.

- 1752 was a busy year for you! In addition to opening the hospital and conducting your lightning experiments, you also founded the **Philadelphia Contributionship**, originally an innovative fire insurance association and now the nation's oldest property insurance company.

- In a 1754 issue of the *Pennsylvania Gazette*, you published (and probably drew) the famous **"Join, or Die" cartoon**, which depicted a snake cut into thirteen sections representing the colonies. Ta-da! The first known political cartoon in American history.

- In 1756, your groundbreaking bill to secure

street lighting and night patrolmen for the city of Philadelphia was passed by the Pennsylvania Assembly.

· Considered America's first diplomat and one of its finest ever, you won French assistance for American independence while on a congressional commission from 1776 to 1778. You became the first **minister to France** in 1778. You are the only person to sign all four of America's major founding documents: the Declaration of Independence, the treaty with France, the Treaty of Paris with England, and the Constitution.

· Toward the end of your life, in 1790, you knew that your work wasn't done. That year, you wrote the **Petition from the Pennsylvania Society for the Abolition of Slavery**, the first petition against slavery to be presented to the US Congress.

BEN: SCIENTIST AND INVENTOR

Your inquisitive mind and practical nature were the driving forces behind your many scientific experiments and creations. If you didn't understand how something worked, you made it your mission to learn. If you thought you could produce tools to improve your lifestyle—and the lifestyles of your fellow colonists— you did. As a matter of fact, many of your inventions are still used today.

- As a young boy, you invented a pair of what we now know as **swimming fins**. Your early version consisted of two oval pieces of wood that you attached to your hands, allowing you to propel yourself underwater. You later tried the same thing with your feet.
- In 1741, you invented the **Franklin stove** as a response to the inadequacies of the common fireplace. Your smart stove was built to contain heat and prevent it from exiting the chimney,

resulting in less wood required, less smoke expended, and more heat. Genius. Years later, in 1758, you even invented a damper for stoves and chimneys.

- Before your creation of the **lightning rod** around 1750, many buildings were susceptible to damage and fire during thunder and electrical storms. Hundreds of people died every year as a result. You conducted a number of experiments and found that if you attached a metal rod to the top of a building, it could intercept the electricity and conduct it to the earth, preventing damage. And though you did not "invent" electricity, your famous **kite experiments** in 1752 proved the existence of electricity in lightning. In addition, you were the first person to use "positive and negative charges," "grounding," "conductor," and "battery" as electrical terms.

- When your brother John suffered from bladder stone pain in 1752, you designed a flexible **urinary catheter** for him.

- In 1761, you created the **glass armonica**, a musical instrument made up of various-sized glasses on a rotating structure. It attracted more than a bit of attention, too. Both Mozart and Beethoven wrote music specifically for your instrument.

- In 1784, as your eyesight worsened and you became both nearsighted and farsighted, you didn't want to be bothered with switching back and forth between different pairs of glasses. So, naturally, you had both pairs' lenses cut in half and then sealed together, creating what may have been the first pair of **bifocal glasses**.

- Although you were quite tall compared to your fellow colonists, you still had trouble reaching books on the highest shelves. As you got older, it became more of a struggle, so in 1786 you designed the **long arm**, a device that's used for multiple purposes today.

BEN: WRITER AND PUBLISHER

Ben, you were a man of many ideas and many, many words. A prolific writer, you penned a myriad of articles, letters, proposals, and treatises during your lifetime. As a young man, you became the sole publisher of the *Pennsylvania Gazette,* much of which you wrote yourself, and you published twenty-six editions of *Poor Richard's Almanack.* Your *Autobiography* is still praised and widely read today. A record of all of your writings can be found at *The Papers of Benjamin Franklin* (franklinpapers.org).

AN EXCERPT FROM YOUR FIRST SILENCE DOGOOD ARTICLE, THE *NEW-ENGLAND COURANT,* 1722

Sir,

It may not be improper in the first place to inform your Readers, that I intend once a Fortnight to present them, by the Help of this Paper, with a short Epistle, which I presume will add somewhat to their Entertainment.

[. . .]

I will not abuse your Patience with a tedious Recital of all the frivolous Accidents of my Life, that happened from this Time until I arrived to Years of Discretion, only inform you that I liv'd a chearful Country Life, spending my leisure Time either in some innocent Diversion with the neighbouring Females, or in some shady Retirement, with the best of Company, Books. Thus I past away thc Timc with a Mixture of Profit and Pleasure, having no affliction but what was imaginary, and created in my own Fancy; as nothing is more common with us Women, than to be grieving for nothing, when we have nothing else to grieve for.

As I would not engross too much of your Paper at once, I will defer the Remainder of my Story until my next Letter; in the mean time desiring your Readers to exercise their Patience, and bear with my Humours now and then, because I shall trouble them but seldom. I am not insensible of the Impossibility of pleasing all, but I would not willingly displease any; and for those who will take Offence where none is intended, they are beneath the Notice of Your Humble Servant,

Silence Dogood

ADVICE FROM *POOR RICHARD'S ALMANACK*

- Light purse, heavy heart. (1733)
- March windy, and April rainy, Makes May the pleasantest month of any. (1733)
- He that lies down with Dogs, shall rise up with fleas. (1733)
- Tongue double, brings trouble. (1733)
- Take this remark from Richard poor and lame, Whate'er's begun in anger ends in shame. (1734)
- Some men grow mad by studying much to know, But who grows mad by studying good to grow. (1734)
- Altho' thy Teacher act not as he preaches, Yet ne'ertheless, if good, do what he teaches. (1734)
- He that waits upon Fortune, is never sure of a Dinner. (1734)
- Look before, or you'll find yourself behind. (1735)
- Be slow in chusing a Friend, slower in changing. (1735)
- Humility makes great men twice honourable. (1735)

- Three may keep a Secret, if two of them are dead. (1735)

LETTER TO DEBORAH, SENT FROM LONDON ON JULY 4, 1771

My dear Child,

I received your kind Letters of April 24. I hope that very bad Cold you had is gone off without any ill Consequences. I have found by a good deal of Experience, that three or four Doses of Bark taken on the first Symptoms of a Cold, will generally put it by. It was a terrible Accident indeed which happened to poor Mr. Rogers and his Family. If I were to build again, I would contrive my House so as to be incapable of burning, which I think very possible and practicable.

I pray God that your Grandson, in whom you seem to take so much Delight, may be preserv'd as a Comfort to you. By your Accounts (and indeed by all the Accounts I have heard) he must be a charming little Fellow. My Love to him. I send him a small Token of it in a new Hat.

You ask me when I think I shall return? I purpose it firmly after one Winter more here. [...]

Your affectionate Husband
B Franklin

Mention to me in your next every thing you want and would have me send or bring with me.

AN EXCERPT FROM YOUR *AUTOBIOGRAPHY,* PART 9, 1771

Selected Virtues with their Precepts:

1. TEMPERANCE. Eat not to Dulness. Drink not to Elevation.
2. SILENCE. Speak not but what may benefit others or yourself. Avoid trifling Conversation.
3. ORDER. Let all your Things have their Places. Let each Part of your Business have its Time.
4. RESOLUTION. Resolve to perform what you ought. Perform without fail what you resolve.
5. FRUGALITY. Make no Expence but to do good to others or yourself: i.e. Waste nothing.

6. INDUSTRY. Lose no Time. Be always employ'd in something useful. Cut off all unnecessary Actions.

7. SINCERITY. Use no hurtful Deceit. Think innocently and justly; and, if you speak, speak accordingly.

8. JUSTICE. Wrong none by doing Injuries or omitting the Benefits that are your Duty.

9. MODERATION. Avoid Extreams. Forbear resenting Injuries so much as you think they deserve.

10. CLEANLINESS. Tolerate no Uncleanness in Body, Cloaths or Habitation.

11. TRANQUILITY. Be not disturbed by trifles, or at Accidents common or unavoidable.

PEN NAMES

You used many pen names—or pseudonyms—throughout your writing life. Though you initially found pen names useful for preserving your anonymity, they eventually functioned as an extension of your wit, satire, and humor. Some even evolved into recurring characters.

- Alice Addertongue
- Anthony Afterwit
- Benevolus
- Busy-Body
- Caelia Shortface and Martha Careful (you wrote letters between these two "women")
- Historicus
- Polly Baker
- Richard Saunders (aka "Poor Richard")
- Silence Dogood

RECOMMENDED READING

BENJAMIN FRANKLIN

Adler, David A. *B. Franklin, Printer.* New York: Holiday House, 2001.

Barretta, Gene. *Now & Ben: The Modern Inventions of Benjamin Franklin.* New York: Henry Holt Books for Young Readers, 2006.

Byrd, Robert. *Electric Ben: The Amazing Life and Times of Benjamin Franklin.* New York: Dial Books for Young Readers, 2012.

Chaplin, Joyce E. *The First Scientific American: Benjamin Franklin and the Pursuit of Genius.* New York: Basic Books, 2006.

Fleming, Candace. *Ben Franklin's Almanac: Being a True Account of the Good Gentleman's Life.* New York: Atheneum Books for Young Readers, 2003.

Fradin, Dennis Brindell. *The Signers: The 56 Stories Behind the Declaration of Independence.* Illustrated by Michael McCurdy. New York: Bloomsbury, 2003.

Franklin, Benjamin. *The Art of Virtue*. Edited by George L. Rogers. Eden Prairie, MN: Acorn Publishing, 1996.

Franklin, Benjamin. *The Autobiography and Other Writings*. New York: Bantam Books, 1982.

Franklin, Benjamin. *Fart Proudly: Writings of Benjamin Franklin You Never Read in School*. Edited by Carl Japikse. Berkeley, CA: Frog Books, 2003.

Franklin, Benjamin, and J. A. Leo Lamay. *Library of America: Benjamin Franklin Book Series*. New York: Library of America, 2005.

Freedman, Russell. *Becoming Ben Franklin: How a Candle-Maker's Son Helped Light the Flame of Liberty*. New York: Holiday House, 2013.

Fritz, Jean. *What's the Big Idea, Ben Franklin?* New York: Putnam & Grosset, 2001.

Giblin, James Cross. *The Amazing Life of Benjamin Franklin*. New York: Scholastic, 2000.

Isaacson, Walter. *Benjamin Franklin: An American Life*. New York: Simon & Schuster, 2004.

Jennings, Francis. *Benjamin Franklin, Politician: The Mask and the Man*. New York: W. W. Norton, 1996.

Krull, Kathleen. *Benjamin Franklin* (Giants of Science). New York: Viking Books for Young Readers, 2013.

Lawson, Robert. *Ben and Me: An Astonishing Life of*

Benjamin Franklin by His Good Mouse Amos. New York: Little, Brown, 1939.

Lepore, Jill. *Book of Ages: The Life and Opinions of Jane Franklin.* New York: Alfred A. Knopf, 2013.

Miller, Brandon Marie. *Benjamin Franklin, American Genius: His Life and Ideas with 21 Activities.* Chicago: Chicago Review Press, 2009.

Morgan, Edmund S. *Benjamin Franklin.* New Haven: Yale University Press, 2002.

Rockliff, Mara. *Mesmerized: How Ben Franklin Solved a Mystery that Baffled All of France.* Somerville: Candlewick Press, 2015.

Rosenstock, Barb. *Ben Franklin's Big Splash. The Mostly True Story of His First Invention.* Honesdale: Calkins Creek, 2014.

Schanzer, Rosalyn. *How Ben Franklin Stole the Lightning.* New York: HarperCollins, 2002.

Schiff, Stacy. *A Great Improvisation: Franklin, France, and the Birth of America.* New York: Henry Holt, 2006.

Smith, Lane. *John, Paul, George, and Ben.* New York: Hyperion Books, 2006.

Van Vleet, Carmella. *Amazing Ben Franklin Inventions You Can Build Yourself.* White River Junction, VT: Nomad Press, 2007.

Wood, Gordon S. *The Americanization of Benjamin Franklin.* New York: Penguin Books, 2005.

AMERICAN REVOLUTION

Aronson, Marc. *The Real Revolution: The Global Story of American Independence.* New York: Clarion Books, 2005.

Freedman, Russell. *Give Me Liberty! The Story of the Declaration of Independence.* New York: Holiday House, 2000.

Freedman, Russell. *Lafayette and the American Revolution.* New York: Holiday House, 2010.

Marrin, Albert. *Thomas Paine: Crusader for Liberty.* New York: Knopf Books for Young Readers, 2014.

Meltzer, Milton. *The American Revolutionaries: A History in Their Own Words, 1750–1800.* New York: Harper-Collins, 1993.

Sheinkin, Steve. *King George: What Was His Problem? The Whole Hilarious Story of the American Revolution.* New York: Square Fish, 2009.

WEBSITES OF INTEREST

Ben Franklin: An Extraordinary Life, an Electric Mind, PBS, pbs.org/benfranklin

Benjamin Franklin: In His Own Words, Library of Congress, loc.gov/exhibits/franklin

Benjamin Franklin's Resume, press.visitphilly.com/releases/benjamin-franklin-s-resume

The Benjamin Franklin Tercentenary, benfranklin300.org

Ben's Guide to the U.S. Government for Kids, bensguide.gpo.gov

The Electric Ben Franklin, ushistory.org/franklin

The Papers of Benjamin Franklin, franklinpapers.org

Penn in the Age of Franklin, 1740–1790, sceti.library.upenn.edu/franklin

WHERE TO "VISIT" BEN TODAY

American Philosophical Society Museum,
Philadelphia, apsmuseum.org

The Bakken Museum, Minneapolis, thebakken.org

Benjamin Franklin House, London,
benjaminfranklinhouse.org

Benjamin Franklin Museum, Philadelphia, nps.gov/
inde/planyourvisit/benjaminfranklinmuseum.htm

Benjamin Franklin National Memorial,
Philadelphia, nps.gov/inde/learn/historyculture/
places-benjaminfranklinnationalmemorial.htm

Franklin Court, Philadelphia, nps.gov/inde/
planyourvisit/franklincourtsites.htm

The Franklin Institute, Philadelphia, fi.edu

Independence Hall, Philadelphia, nps.gov/inde/
planyourvisit/independencehall.htm

Smithsonian National Postal Museum, Washington,
DC, postalmuseum.si.edu

IMAGE CREDITS

SOURCES

Chaplin, Joyce E. *The First Scientific American: Benjamin Franklin and the Pursuit of Genius.* New York: Basic Books, 2006.

Franklin, Benjamin. *The Art of Virtue.* Edited by George L. Rogers. Eden Prairie, MN: Acorn Publishing, 1996.

Franklin, Benjamin. *The Autobiography and Other Writings.* New York: Bantam Books, 1982.

Franklin, Benjamin. *Fart Proudly: Writings of Benjamin Franklin You Never Read in School.* Edited by Carl Japikse. Berkeley, CA: Frog Books, 2003.

Isaacson, Walter. *Benjamin Franklin: An American Life.* New York: Simon & Schuster, 2004.

Jennings, Francis. *Benjamin Franklin, Politician: The Mask and the Man.* New York: W. W. Norton, 1996.

Lepore, Jill. *Book of Ages: The Life and Opinions of Jane Franklin.* New York: Alfred A. Knopf, 2013.

Morgan, Edmund S. *Benjamin Franklin.* New Haven: Yale University Press, 2002.

Schiff, Stacy. *A Great Improvisation: Franklin, France, and the Birth of America.* New York: Henry Holt, 2006.

Wood, Gordon S. *The Americanization of Benjamin Franklin.* New York: Penguin Books, 2005.

NOTES

The notes below show where we found our quotations. No, we did NOT make them up! Unless we say otherwise, "Franklin" means *The Autobiography and Other Writings*. FYI: Franklin-era style can look weird to modern readers, so we occasionally clarify by putting punctuation or spelling in line with modern usage.

Choice I—1723: Oh, Brother!

"thought, probably with reason": Franklin, 19.

"too much of it": Isaacson, 33.

"Of all knaves": Isaacson, 32.

"little better than dunces" and "as great blockheads": Isaacson, 31.

"Perhaps I was": Franklin, 20.

"Let thy child's": Lepore, 20.

"a little obnoxious": Franklin, 20.

Choice II—1727: Fresh in Philly!

"three great puffy rolls": Franklin, 24.

"thought I made": Franklin, 24.

"What shall we think": Franklin, 38.

"I began to suspect": Franklin, 46.

"sense being preferable": Franklin, 467.

"Sin is not hurtful": Morgan, 19.

"A virtuous heretic": Wood, 30.

"established for mutual improvement": Wood, 195.

"The good men may do": Isaacson, 102.

"The present little sacrifice": Franklin, 72.

"To pour forth benefits": Isaacson, 103.

Choice III—1730: "The Odd Half of a Pair of Scissors"

"unfortunate situation": Isaacson, 63.

"resembles the odd half": Franklin, *Fart Proudly,* 27.

"resented": Franklin, 62.

"genteel new suit": Franklin, 28.

"Keep your eyes wide open": Isaacson, 75.

"Don't you know" and "honor and obey": Isaacson, 81.

Choice IV—1748: Act Two

"When nature gave": Isaacson, 84.

"to this day": Lepore, 68.

"When men differ": Isaacson, 66.

"cheerfully service": Isaacson, 67.

"ample amends": Franklin, 94.

"I am excessive" and "the printer has offered":
     Franklin, 182.

"My printer": Isaacson, 97.

"Early to bed" and other Poor Richard examples:
     Isaacson, 99.

"He that has once": Franklin, 95.

"middling people": Isaacson, 125.

"Being thus unprotected" and "This association is
     founded": Isaacson, 126.

"independent of this government" and "He is a
     dangerous": Wood, 69.

"the most magically magical": Schiff, 48.

"What signifies philosophy": Isaacson, 130.

"As we enjoy": Franklin, 108.

"little black spot": Franklin, 78.

"I cannot boast," "Disguise it," and "I would probably
     be": Franklin, 84–85.

"A perfect character": Franklin, 82.

"The use of money": Morgan, 25.

"I would rather have it said": Isaacson, 127.

"Content and riches": Morgan, 25.

"Dost thou love life?": Franklin, 186.

"Human [happiness] is produced": Franklin, 118.

Choice V—1754: United Colonies of America?

"the human serpents" and "the rattlesnake gives":
    Franklin, 220.

"six nations of ignorant savages": Wood, 73.

"It is supposed": Isaacson, 161.

"the ill consequences": Wood, 76–77.

Choice VI—1765: Death and Taxes

"In this world": Isaacson, 463.

"Who would have thought it?": Isaacson, 168.

"at times turns white": Jennings, 144.

"more slavish than slavery": Isaacson, 169.

"Those who would give up": Jennings, 117.

"had been a member" and "The people happen":
    Wood, 80.

"home to England": Wood, 82.

"There are very few": Isaacson, 183.

"poor defenseless creatures," etc.: Isaacson, 211.

"We are in your hands": Wood, 107.

"I wish some good angel": Morgan, 143.

"We might [as] well": Isaacson, 223.

"When you and I were at Albany": Wood, 110.

"Idleness and pride": Morgan, 153.

"informing, explaining, consulting": Wood, 117.

"I was but a bad speaker": Franklin, 85.

"led by a thread": Morgan, 157.

"will not find a rebellion": Isaacson, 230.

"the people might suppose": Isaacson, 223.

"a more . . . thorough contempt": Wood, 92.

"Doing an injury": Schiff, 181.

Choice VII—1772: A "Small Leak"?

"our North American subjects": Wood, 122.

"hold fast [our] loyalty": Wood, 130.

"in England of being too much": Isaacson, 246.

"dissatisfied distress": Isaacson, 240.

"I find myself growing": Wood, 132.

"your a feck shonet wife": Wood, 131.

"nothing was more common": Isaacson, 254.

"fish and visitors stink": Lepore, 22.

"I shall find myself a stranger": Franklin letter to
    Deborah Franklin, April 6, 1773, *The Papers of
    Benjamin Franklin*, franklinpapers.org.

"There must be an abridgment": Morgan, 186.

"out of zeal" and "take nobody's business":
    Isaacson, 62.

"Three may keep a secret": Isaacson, 99.

"Then, thought I" and "So convenient a thing":
    Franklin, 32–33.

"A small leak will sink": Franklin, 189.

"To get over this": Franklin, 254.

"Every affront is not worth": Wood, 143.

"some men of worth," "bartering away," and "most if
    not all": Franklin letter to Thomas Cushing,
    December 2, 1772, *The Papers of Benjamin Franklin*,
    franklinpapers.org.

"their resentment against England": Morgan, 197.

"It is words only": Isaacson, 272.

**Choice VIII—1775: "There Never Was a Good War or
a Bad Peace"**

"extensive dominions": Franklin, 240.

"have held up" and "I grew tired": Lepore, 163.

"incense the Mother Country": Isaacson, 276.

"Thou base, ungrateful": Wood, 146.

"act of violent injustice": Isaacson, 275.

"forfeited all the respect" and "man of letters":
     Isaacson, 277.

"one of the bitterest": Morgan, 217.

"the lowest of Mankind" and "to govern a herd":
     Wood, 150.

"There never was a good war": Isaacson, 392, 417.

"It is an honester": Wood, 161.

"But you, who are" and "Honored father":
     Isaacson, 282.

"We have no favors": Isaacson, 153.

"He does not hesitate": Wood, 155.

"You are a Member of Parliament": Wood, 157.

"Britain having begun a war": Isaacson, 301.

"Britain, at the expense": Isaacson, 303.

"In my conscience I believe": Morgan, 273.

"Do you think it prudent": Morgan, 221.

"As they could not get": Franklin, *Fart Proudly,* 100.

"no natural or religious reason": Isaacson, 307–8.

"obnoxious, suspected, and unpopular": Isaacson, 310.

"There must be no pulling": Isaacson, 313.

"quite unexpected news" and "set the colonies":
     Isaacson, 293–94.

"unruly soldiers": Isaacson, 323.

"I am old and good for nothing": Isaacson, 321.

Choice IX—1778: Celebrity, Secrets, and Spies

"The numbers sold are incredible": Isaacson, 327.

"chief of the rebels": Schiff, 21.

"simplicity and innocence" and "unalterable serenity":
Isaacson, 327–28.

"As [Franklin] is a subtle": Schiff, 24.

"It is not a truth": Isaacson, 340.

"To injure England": Schiff, 78.

"England is the natural enemy": Isaacson, 337.

"One can connive": Schiff, 10.

"A minister's residence": Schiff, 60.

"Instead of Howe taking Philadelphia": Isaacson, 342.

"All the better": Schiff, 63.

"In sowing suspicions": Morgan, 257.

"no troops ever fought so well": Schiff, 146.

"Tyranny is so generally established": Isaacson, 339.

"If some of the many enemies": Franklin letter to
Samuel Wharton, June 17, 1780, *The Papers of
Benjamin Franklin*, franklinpapers.org.

"the Founding Father of Covert Action": Central
Intelligence Agency website, cia.gov/news-
information/featured-story-archive/benjamin-
franklin.html.

"simply this": Schiff, 44–45.

"They play us off": Schiff, 132.

"give it a little revenge": Wood, 191.

Choice X—1782: Let's Make a Deal

"This is the civilest nation": Isaacson, 329.

"I do not find": Isaacson, 367.

"women and children": Isaacson, 352.

"that gaiety and gallantry": Isaacson, 362.

"She had a little lapdog": Isaacson, 365.

"Let us revenge ourselves": Schiff, 233.

"I have not yet begun to fight!": Isaacson, 390.

"They quarrel *at* me": Schiff, 207.

"have a monopoly of reputation": Isaacson, 351.

"no other sentiments": Schiff, 316.

"mongrel character," "unlimited ambition," and
    "panting for glory": Isaacson, 410.

"the King has not stood": Schiff, 248.

"I have passed" and "honor sufficient": Isaacson, 396.

"I call this continuance an honor": Isaacson, 398.

"as zealous and patriotic": Isaacson, 397.

"the ravings of a certain": Wood, 195.

"coop us up": Isaacson, 409.

"[He] has gone on": Isaacson, 411.

"All wars are follies": Isaacson, 417.

"The *form* may perhaps": Wood, 160.

"abrupt" and "agreeable to the King": Wood, 415.

"we shall be but poorly paid": Wood, 416–17.

"Lafayette, we are here": Schiff, 166.

"As we played pretty equally": Franklin, 92.

"Ah, we do not take kings" and "The game of chess":
     Isaacson, 372.

Choice XI—1787: Liberty for All?

"people do not enquire": Isaacson, 423.

"What is the use": Isaacson, 421.

"No one can replace him": Thomas Jefferson letter to
     Reverend William Smith, February 19, 1791, *The
     Papers of Thomas Jefferson,* founders.archives.gov.

"In all cases of public service": Wood, 217.

"Declarations of a fixed opinion": Isaacson, 449.

"children become proud": Franklin, 224.

"every slave is by nature": Franklin, 222.

"higher opinion of the natural capacities":
     Chaplin, 181.

"this pestilential detestable traffic": Franklin,
     "The Sommersett Case and the Slave Trade,"
     June 18, 1772, *The Papers of Benjamin Franklin,*
     franklinpapers.org.

"this Constitution because I expect": Franklin, 251.

"slavery is such an atrocious debasement" and "has long been treated": Wood, 227.

"the blessings of Liberty": Wood, 228.

"brought into a land": Isaacson, 466.

"Let All Men Know Thee"

"mighty genius": Wood, 230.

"The Body of B. Franklin": Franklin, 270.

"Let all men know thee": Isaacson, 101.

"a bird of bad moral character": Isaacson, 423.

"improve the common stock": Franklin, "A Proposal for Promoting Useful Knowledge," May 14, 1743, *The Papers of Benjamin Franklin,* franklinpapers.org.

A NOTE FROM THE AUTHORS

How did this book come to be? We've always shared a love for history: Tom studied ancient civilizations in college, and Leila has been entranced by stories, especially true ones, for as long as she can remember. The word "story" comes from a word that also means "history," so it makes sense that the best stories often come from real life.

We'd been talking about writing a kids' book together as a fun father-daughter project, and what could be more up our alley than a biography? But we didn't want to do just any biography: to us there's nothing more fascinating about someone than his or her key life decisions. Ben Franklin's choices not only changed the course of his life (and of history), but also showed who he really was. We figured, too, that our target readers were at the age to start making real choices of their own (about friends, schools, hobbies, and other major issues). To kids who are beginning to take control of their own lives, we thought walking through the decisions Ben made in his life, and even guessing what they'd be, could be a lot more interesting than just reading about stuff that happened to him.

Fun fact: some of you may have already enjoyed *It's Up to You, Abe Lincoln,* but we actually wrote this book first! Here's how we did it. We began by reading up on Ben. Then each of us picked out life choices that seemed especially dramatic, revealing, or historically significant. (Our lists overlapped less than we expected.) The hardest part, but one of the most enjoyable, was narrowing our combined list down to just eleven decision points. That helped us focus when we did deeper research: digging into a bunch of books (especially the ones that Ben wrote himself—he was so funny!), exploring online resources like the Franklin Papers database, and (best of all) traveling together to the town where Ben spent most of his life: Philadelphia. We toured the Benjamin Franklin Museum, a re-creation of his old printing shop, a tavern where he used to hang out, Independence Hall (where he helped create both the Declaration of Independence and the US Constitution), and other amazing places.

Next came the actual writing. We divvied up the chapters for that crucial first draft. We'd each write sections on our own, then swap and edit, then swap again and edit some more—and so on, until we thought each chapter truly had both of us in it. Toward the end, we had fun adding the final touches, like chapter titles and illustration ideas, to make the manuscript ready for our wonderful editor, Phoebe Yeh.

We'll be thrilled if kids enjoy reading this book as much as we enjoyed writing it together!

TOM AND LEILA HIRSCHFELD

Go inside the mind (and stovepipe hat!) of Abe Lincoln.
Turn the page for more big decisions and bigger laughs!

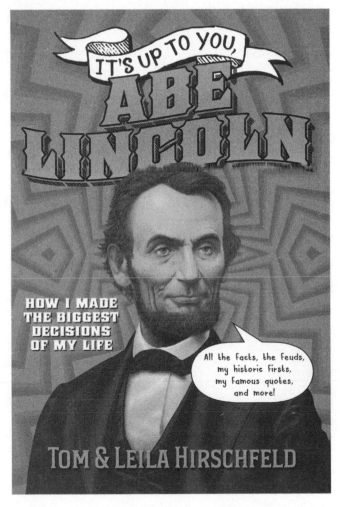

OUT OF BUSINESS

THE CHALLENGE

YOUR STORE WENT BUST, LEAVING you with huge debts. How can you get out of this fix?

THE BACKSTORY

LATER, WHEN YOU'RE FAMOUS, YOU'LL downplay your early years of poverty, dismissing your own story as "short and simple." Really, Abraham? In fact, your home life was pretty complicated, with many moves, deaths, and deprivations that played a major role in producing the anything-but-simple person you would become.

Your dad's father, and *his* father, each lived in at least three different parts of the country. Your dad, Thomas Lincoln, followed their example, searching for new opportunities time and again as the American frontier shifted westward. Your dad tended to move once the neighborhood became too settled, so you spent your growing years more or less in the wilderness.

THOMAS LINCOLN

Your older cousin Dennis Hanks, who lived with you, will remember (when you're famous) how your dad covered you and your mom, Nancy, with a bearskin after she gave birth to you in Kentucky. As with all your family homes, your first was a log cabin built mostly by your dad.

Dennis will tell how you spent most of your boyhood wandering barefoot: "Abe was right out in the woods, about as soon's he was weaned, fishin' in the crick, set-tin' traps fur rabbits an' muskrats, goin' on coon-hunts with Tom an' me an' the dogs, follerin' up bees to find bee-trees, an' [plantin'] corn fur his pappy. Mighty interestin' life fur a boy, but thar was a good many chances he wouldn't live to grow up."

The brightest part of your Kentucky years was your sister, Sarah, two years older, who rocked your cradle before you could walk and, after, taught you to pick blueberries and fetch kindling. When you were six, she refused to go to her one-room schoolhouse unless "little Abe" could go with her. (As an adult, FYI, you'll usually go by Abraham.) On the way, Sarah held your hand so you would not be scared; once there, she helped you learn your first numbers and letters. "Yessiree, Sairy an' Abe was more'n brother an' sister," Dennis will say. "[They] was best friends."

ON THE MOVE

AT AGE SEVEN, YOU MOVED to Indiana, an even wilder place—so wild that you'd one day write a poem about it:

> *When first my father settled here,*
> *'Twas then the frontier line:*
> *The panther's scream filled night with*
> * fear*
> *And bears preyed on the swine.*

You had your share of run-ins with the local wildlife, but you were never big on hunting it. Soon after arriving in Indiana, you shot a wild turkey on the wing (through a hole in the roof—nice aim for a seven-year-old!). You raced outside proudly, but he looked so beautiful lying there dead, you felt terrible. Ever after, you refused to kill any large game—a highly unusual attitude on the frontier.

You yourself almost died twice, once when you fell into a stream (luckily, a friend fished you out with a branch) and once when the family mare kicked you in the head. You were swatting her so she'd go faster but instead got yourself "apparently killed for a time."

Your folks never had much money. You spent your boyhood in ragged buckskins that you constantly outgrew, so your shinbones often stuck out beyond your pants. (In cold weather, you wore a cap of squirrel or raccoon skin.)

But the greatest lack you felt, the biggest gap in your life, was knowledge. You never got more than a few months of schooling at a time (less than a year altogether), and you never had enough *books.*

In Indiana you would tell Dennis, "The things I want to know is in books. My best friend is the man who'll git me one," but most folks couldn't help you. Few could read themselves. One neighbor would see you writing "words and sentences wherever he could. . . . He scrawled them with charcoal, he scored them in the dust, in the sand, in the snow—anywhere and everywhere."

DIDYA KNOW?

Abe was a huge fan of the Bard. He always enjoyed the theater and was especially fond of Shakespeare's *Macbeth.*

You could even earn a few cents writing letters for folks,

a reward that only increased your appetite for learning.

Over time, kind adults loaned or gave you copies of *Aesop's Fables, Robinson Crusoe,* the Bible, a biography of George Washington, and other works. According to Dennis, you were a "constant and I may say stubborn reader." You grew to love stories of all kinds: when you were reading *The Arabian Nights* to Dennis and Sarah, Dennis called it a pack of lies, to which you replied, "Mighty darned good lies."

You would memorize your favorite passages, writing them in a copybook or (if you had no paper) on boards. You also kept up with your arithmetic, scrawling these immortal lines in one math notebook that survives:

> *Abraham Lincoln*
> *his hand and pen*
> *he will be good but*
> *god knows when.*

You *were* good, at least at remembering what you learned. In your words, your mind was like some hard metal: it was "very hard to scratch anything on it and almost impossible once you get it there to rub it out."